MW01126927

FUN – COOKING FOR CHILDREN

This book, written specially for children of all ages, is a fun-filled introduction to a most creative and satisfying hobby --- cooking. There are simple "projects" for the junior-most cook just as there are more advanced ones for the innovative teenager.

Every recipe is minutely detailed, simply written and complimented charmingly by amusing illustrations, to guide the child through every step of cooking all kinds of favourite foods. The menu includes Sandwiches, Drinks, Salads, Snacks, Baked Delights and even simple mini-meals. A detailed introduction to kitchen aids has been thoughtfully planned to include procedures adults normally take for granted -- how to break an egg, how to separate it, how to sift flour, how to chop vegetables and fruits. Apart from aiming to make the young cook confident and independent in the kitchen, the book accents the fun and enjoyment of cooking for friends, family or just oneself. Some very special recipes have been created revolving around fairy-tales, and other story-book characters. Children are sure to enjoy cooking from this volume. Parents too may not be immune to its charms!

FUN-COOKING FOR CHILDREN

Rohini Singh

 UBSPD

UBS Publishers' Distributors Ltd.

New Delhi • Bombay • Bangalore • Madras
Calcutta • Patna • Kanpur • London

UBS Publishers' Distributors Ltd.
5 Ansari Road, New Delhi-110 002
Bombay Bangalore Madras Calcutta
Patna Kanpur London

© Rohini Singh

First Published 1993

Cover design : UBS Art Studio
Illustrations : Kamla Singh & Taarini Chopra

Composed in 11 pt. Bookman and printed at Rajkamal Electric
Press, B-35/9 G.T. Karnal Road Industrial Area, Delhi.

Contents

CONTENTS

CONTENTS

Contents

Rohini Singh

Isn't it exciting when you buy a new toy or even a new gadget or utensil? You can hardly wait to reach home, to tear open the wrapper and examine it from all angles. To make you feel even cleverer and prouder of yourself, some papers usually tumble out of the box. Congratulations, they say, you are now the proud owner of whatever it is you've bought. They go on to tell you (as if you needed any more convincing!) how lucky you are and how much fun you're now going to have with it. Well, you know, I almost feel like doing the same thing. I feel like saying Congratulations! You are now the proud owner of a ticket to fun. I'm so glad you're deciding to experiment in the kitchen and I assure you you're going to enjoy yourself thoroughly. What is more, I hope this will be your introduction to a life-time hobby that is not only fun but is also so very creative and satisfying.

Are there, by the way, some of you who have never yet experimented in the kitchen? Perhaps you weren't allowed in because it is considered dangerous? Well, you know, it's about as dangerous as learning to ride a bicycle. Just as you may have a fall from your cycle or you may knock into something and hurt yourself, so with cooking. You can cut yourself, because you often have to use a knife for cutting and chopping, or you may touch something that's too hot and burn yourself. But then as in cycling, there are some things you must learn so you can keep yourself safe and still have fun. Once you can 'balance' yourself in the kitchen as you learn to do on your cycle, there is absolutely nothing to be fearful of. Just take your time, start with the easier recipes and I am sure you will soon be cutting and chopping and cooking wonderfully well.

Of course, you do know what the first day of cycling is like? You start with a small cycle to begin with. Perhaps it has extra wheels on the side to keep you steady. Even then, you feel a little wobbly and unsure and you're glad if some-one holds you for a while and runs along beside you as you learn. Well, let the same rule apply in the kitchen. If you're unsure and a little wobbly, let an adult help you get your balance and you'll soon be whizzing along comfortably without help.

There's another reason you may have been shooed away from the kitchen. Perhaps the adults in your house were sure you would make a mess that would take a long while to clear? Well, that's not wholly unfair, you know. I can tell you that it's very easy to make a mess and leave it that way hoping someone else—a fairy godmother—will appear to make it all vanish! Now that's something you have to promise me you won't do. You have to promise the adults in your house too, specially the person whose kitchen you will be using. But once you do that, once you turn the page, in fact, and take some time to read and digest some simple rules that you need to keep in mind, I am sure you will have no problem at all getting permission to use the kitchen and the many things in it. And then, I can tell you, you're in for a really great adventure. And I'm in it with you all the way.

Have a delectable, scrumptious, luscious journey. Say those words out loud (they all mean delicious, you know) roll them on your tongue; get used to the sound of them because I'm sure you're going to hear them often as we set out on this roller coaster, savouring the flavours of fun.

Let's go !

Your
Rohini Aunty

RULES TO KEEP IN MIND WHEN YOU'RE COOKING

You do want to become a good, efficient cook, don't you? Well, here are some of the things you must keep in mind.

1. The first step of course is to decide on the recipe you want to try out. Read it carefully, and see that you understand every step of it.

2. Now get together all the things you will need for it. Shop for the things you don't have. You wouldn't enjoy dashing out in the middle of making your recipe to get something from the market, would you? When you're ready to start, lay out all the things on the counter—that means ingredients (things you need to cook the recipe) plus all the dishes, spoons, knives etc.

3. Now do something you normally don't like to. Wash your hands! And wash them well.

4. Put on your apron so your clothes aren't splashed with blobs of chocolate or stains of oil.

5. If you have long hair, tie it up. You know how upsetting it is when you get a hair coming out of your food?

6. Now get to work. In other words, have fun. Keep your recipe in front of you, preferably with a book-mark in it so you don't follow two recipes at

5

a time. Can you imagine chocolate cake with *chaat masala* in it? Better still, copy it out before you start and stick it up where you're working.

7. When you've finished, clear up. Wash up the dirty dishes, if you're expected to otherwise pile them up neatly in the sink. Clean the counter tops with a sponge or cloth meant for the purpose. If you prefer, you can lay a newspaper on the counter before you start which you can then simply throw away. Put away all the gadgets you may have used where they belong. That is the only price you have to pay for the fun you've had. It's not asking too much, is it?

Just to help you remember all that I've said, I've made up a little poem for you. You can copy it out and stick it up in a little corner of the kitchen. Here it is :

THE GOOD COOK'S POEM

Wash your hands. Go on, scrub!
You wouldn't want germs in your grub!
Give your recipe a nice long read
Get together all the things you need.
Put on your apron. Now you're ready,
You know what works best? Slow and steady!
And when your cooking for the day is done,
Remember what I said about the price of fun?
Yes, leave the place all neat and clean.
Wash and wipe—you know what I mean.
Well done! Great! I'm proud of you.
And I know some others will be too!

Have you digested all this? Now let me introduce you to some of your helpers in the kitchen.

6

MEET THE HELPERS

T his is the biggest helper of all—a mixi. She may also be known by a more important sounding

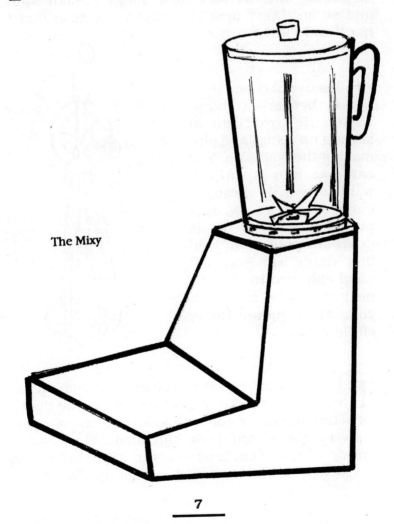

The Mixy

name—a food processor. She can grind, chop, mince, puree (which means make a paste) but before she does all that for you, you must get to know her. Tell whoever usually uses her to show you what buttons to press and blades to fix to make her whirr and purr and hum. Also, be careful not to do any of the things she doesn't like for example, keeping her on too long or putting into her very hard things without water and so on. Don't upset her and you'll soon find it hard to do without her.

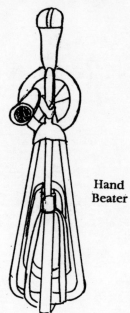

Hand Beater

This useful character is a beater—a hand beater. He's excellent at stirring up things and also making them smooth. You can use him when you want to beat up cream or curds or even an egg. Just put him with his hands down into your bowl, hold him steady with your left hand and turn the handle he has on the side with your right hand. He is efficient.

This is his more modern cousin. Plug him into an electric point and watch him go! Yes, he does it all better and faster and with less effort on your part. I'm very fond of him. I use him almost every day for one or other reason. If he exists in your kitchen, beg to use him and promise to clean him up after. Again,

as with the mixi, let whoever knows about him, tell
you his likes and dislikes.

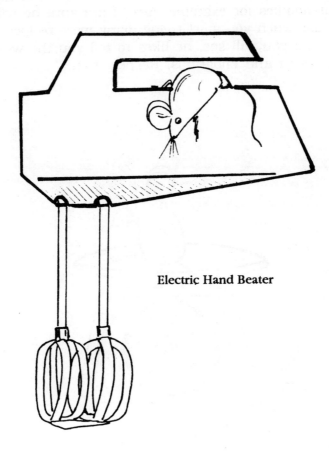

Electric Hand Beater

T his is a weighing scale, that precise old man who's responsible for all your recipes coming out just perfectly time after time. You will not need to take his help too often since most of the measurements in this book are in cups. Yet, you should know him when you meet him, specially since he will measure out noodles for example. Also, I am sure he will be of use when you start trying many more recipes.

As you will see, he likes to tell you the weights in grams and kilograms. Respect him.

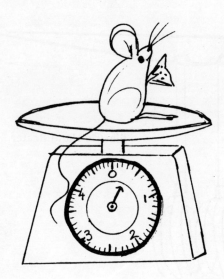

T his is a set of measuring cups and spoons. If you don't have them, get them before you start if you want good results. If you don't want to get the whole set, get at least one cup and you can work out other measures from it, for example, a half cup, quarter cup (half of half!) and one-third cup. Similarly, with the spoons. You will have a tea-spoon at home but you might like to get the proper measuring tablespoon.

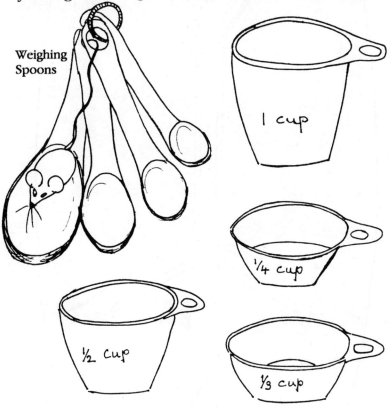

Weighing
Spoons

1 cup

¼ cup

½ cup

⅓ cup

Measuring Cups

11

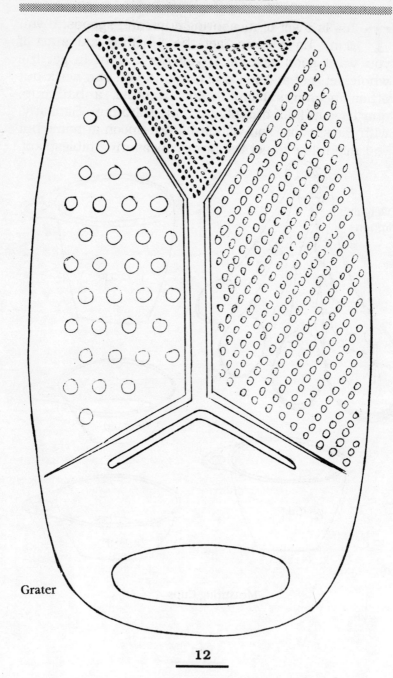

Grater

12

This delicate gadget does a lot of useful work. She grates your cheese, onions, ginger, garlic, carrots, cucumber, in fact anything at all that needs grating. She can do a fine or not-so-fine a job. Look at the holes on her body and you will understand how. All you do is hold whatever you want against her and rub gently. Keep a plate under to hold the grated stuff, but be careful you don't get bits of grated finger too!

You might sometime need to ask this strong man for help, when you want lemon juice minus the seeds. You might be feeling like having a glass of *Nimbu Pani* for instance or you just might need some lemon juice over your *chaat*. Just put your lemon down into the cup of his hand, press down with the other handle and in a trice, you have juiced your lemon. Of course you have to remember to keep a glass or bowl underneath.

Lemon Squeezer

13

Now let me introduce you to another goody-goody girl. She will help you to separate good from bad or to be more precise, clean from dirty. Put whatever you want cleaned into her—it could be flour, (*maida*), gramflour (*besan*), semolina (*sooji*). Shake her—the clean stuff will go down into a plate while she holds onto all the bits of dirt for you. She may not always be this shape. She could be fatter and rounder but I can assure you she'll do the work just as well.

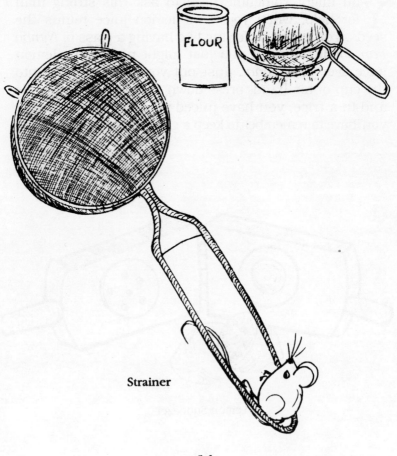

FLOUR

Strainer

N ow, meet this cheerful fellow who likes to whistle while he works. I'm sure you hear him at it almost every day. He helps you cook faster than you would be able to do otherwise. I might ask some of you—the older ones—to use him. You may need to ask someone at home to show you how he likes his top fixed before he starts work.

Pressure Cooker

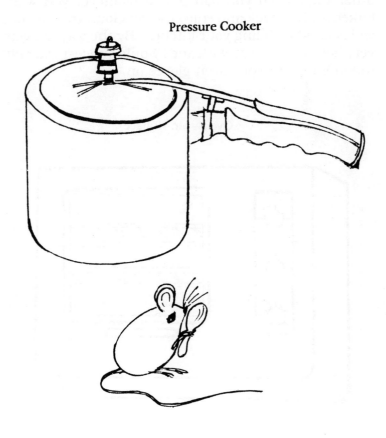

A nd this is another one of my helpers that I'm very fond of. I call him my Hotface. He is the one without whom you wouldn't have chocolate cakes and biscuits and baked spaghetti and lots of other good things of life. To use him, you must plug him into an electric socket and then set on him the temperature you want him to heat up to. He'll tell you when he's ready usually by winking with the little light he has on him or in some other way. Then you can put in whatever you want baked and sit back and enjoy the delicious aromas that will soon start filling your kitchen. By the way, he gets very hot when he's at work and I would suggest you only touch him with your oven-gloves on.

Oven -- Mr. Hotface

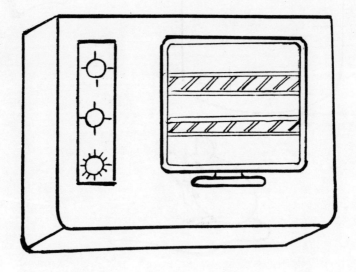

H ere is another little gadget I can't do without. She has a clock on her face and would you believe, she keeps the time for me, telling me when my cooking ought to be over. All I have to do is set the time on her—35 minutes for a cake, for example— and then I can go off and do something else. When 35 minutes are over, she rings and reminds me to come and take my cake out of the oven. Isn't that wonderful? But for her, I might have lots more burnt cakes to feel sorry about. Use her too if you have her, specially if you are often absent minded!

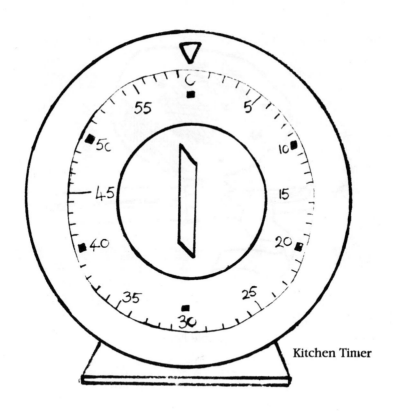

Kitchen Timer

T his slim little gadget with a sharp steel head and a funny punky hairstyle comes into her own when you need to peel vegetables or hard fruits— potatoes, cucumber, pears—and she does it so smoothly and easily. Hold her blade against the vegetable and pull gently towards yourself. The peel is neatly pulled away, without taking too much of the fruit or vegetable with it. You will be thankful for her help when you're making salads or fruit *chaat*.

Vegetable Peeler

And then there are knives and spoons in different sizes and shapes. I am sure you know most of them well. As we go along in the recipes, you will see how much we take them for granted.

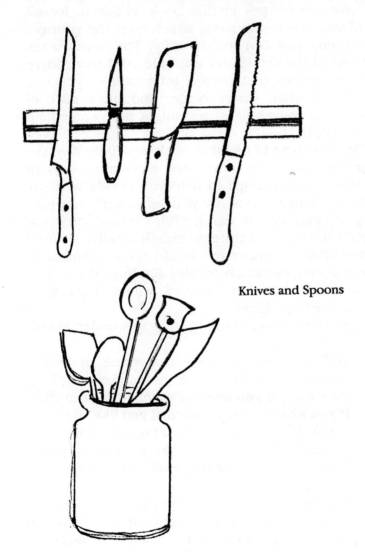

Knives and Spoons

HOW TO USE THIS BOOK

T here are recipes in this book, children, for all of you. There are some which even the younger ones among you can make easily. The Sandwiches and most of the drinks, for example. And then, there are other recipes that need a little care so you can make them when you're bigger and more sure of yourself. For some stages, you might need some help from an adult.

The best way to use this book, specially if you're under ten, would be to ask one of your parents to look through the recipe to help you decide whether or not you can do it all by yourself. Don't be upset if they say you have to wait a while—before you know it, you'll have grown up enough! Generally, I would imagine children under ten would not be allowed to make the recipes which involve lighting of the gas. Kids who are over ten however, would, I am sure have no such problem.

Here are some other things you may wonder about:

1. You may sometimes see in a recipe, under the list of things you will need, the name of something followed by **if you like.** For example, 1 green chilli, **if you like** or some mustard, if **you like.** This only means use it if you like chilli-hot food or the taste of mustard. If you don't like it, you can safely leave it out and your recipe will still be successful.

2. Similarly, you may sometimes see before the thing you are using an amount which is not definite. For example, **1-2 teaspoons sugar** or

salt. Again, this is to allow you to use as much or as little as you want because you know some people like things very sweet or very salty while others don't. So this is something you will have to decide as you go along.

3. You will also often see oven temperatures that differ like this : **Bake for 35-45 minutes, or till done.** This happens because ovens differ-some are more efficient than others and bake in 35 minutes while others do it in 45 or more. So you have to get to know your own oven and its timings. Remember to note them down in your book so you don't have any problem the second time around.

4. Sometimes you may see quantities like this that might confuse you —**a pinch, a squeeze, a dot.** Let me explain them to you—a pinch is literally that. Form your fingers into pinching position. Now imagine picking up some *masala* in that position. That's a pinch. A squeeze, again is just a squeeze—a little more than a few drops. A dot is a dot. Its just that these measures are too small to put into teaspoons so you better learn them as they really are!

5. You might see this * next to one of the things you need in your recipe. This only means I want to tell you something more about it, which you will usually find at the end of the recipe.

6. By the way, when you measure out any thing, remember it should be measured flat. That

21

means, the tablespoon or teaspoon should not be heaped full but the thing you are measuring should come up to the edge in a flat line. This is easy to do with dry things like sugar or flour but it is not so easy with butter. To get your measurements right, take the butter in the spoon and, smoothen it flat with a knife.

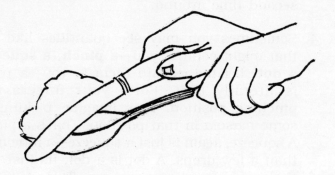

Measuring -- by levelling with a knife

OTHER THINGS YOU OUGHT TO KNOW

H ere are some things you will need to do often and I'd like to teach you exactly how to go about them.

1. **Breaking an egg:** Its easy when you know how, otherwise you can make a terrible mess. Hold the egg in your left hand, and crack it smartly with a sharp knife. Holding it over a bowl, the crack facing downwards, gently press the two halves apart, and let the egg fall into the bowl below.

2. **Separating an egg:** Put the broken egg into a plate. Take a small *katori* (dish) and upturn it over the yolk (that's the yellow part). Into another bowl or plate, tip the white while the yellow stays trapped under the *katori*. Simple, isn't it? Not all adults know how to do it quite as well.

3. **Sifting Flour:** This you will need to do whenever you use flour, to separate any rubbish—little stones, hair, even bits of string sometimes, insects—it has in it. To do it, take a large plate. Put it down on the counter top. Holding the strainer over the plate, pour the flour into it, and shake gently. The flour will fall onto the plate, the rubbish will remain behind. Just be careful, you're not shaking it so hard that the flour is landing on the counter-top instead of in the plate!

4. **Making onion chopping less tearful:** After you peel the onion, drop it into a bowl of water. If you let it sit in the bowl for about 15 minutes, you will find it loses some of its power to make you cry as your chop it.

23

To chop it, hold it steady on the chopping board with your left hand and neatly slice it in half with your right hand. Now put one half, cut side down on the board and slice long lines across it, keeping the onion intact. Now cut the other way so the second set of lines cuts across the first set. You need a little practice but I'm sure you'll soon be perfect!

5. **Chopping a tomato:** Put the tomato down on a chopping board. Hold it steady with your left hand. With the tip of a sharp knife, make a cut in the top. Put the blade of the knife in the cut and slice the tomato. Don't press down. Slice by moving the knife back and forth. Cut in halves, then quarters. This is what you will need for salad. To cut smaller bits, slice the half in strips and the strips in little bits. You would do exactly the same if you want to **cut a lemon** in half.

6. **Chopping a green chilli:** Lay the chilli on th chopping board. Holding it steady with your left hand cut in thin slices with a sharp knife. Keep moving your left hand back, out of the way, as you go along. You may remove the seeds if you like, before you use the chilli.

Before I end, an apology to my young friends who are left-handed. I am sorry all the instructions here are for kids who generally use their right hands to do most things including write. Please, if you use your left hand instead, just reverse the directions.

A ll the oven temperatures in the book are in centigrade. If at your house you have an oven that prefers to function in Fahrenheit, here's a table to help you convert.

121°C	=	250°F
135°C	=	275°F
149°C	=	300°F
163°C	=	325°F
177°C	=	350°F
191°C	=	375°F
204°C	=	400°F
218°C	=	425°F
232°C	=	450°F
246°C	=	475°F

Now, don't you think it's about time we stopped talking and started cooking ? Lets get on with it.

FUN WITH SANDWICHES

S andwiches **are** satisfying. They're quick to make, good to eat and can be as creative as you are. Yes, indeed, they can be a lot of fun as you will see by the time you come to the end of this chapter. However, you know something, even though there's really nothing difficult about making a sandwich, not everyone knows how to make a really good one. I want you to learn how. Shall I share some secrets with you?

1. Well, first of all you have to cut the crusts off the slices of bread and you have to do it neatly. You need a chopping board and a sharp knife. Lay the slice of bread on the board. Hold it down flat with your left hand and gently cut off the crust on the right. Don't press down too hard or pull because if the bread is fresh, as it should be, you will make a mess. Do it gently, and if you move your knife back and forth like you may have seen a carpenter do when he's sawing wood, you will find it much easier.

2. As you keep cutting, you must keep the slices covered with a wet napkin otherwise they will dry out before you know it, specially in summer. You must have seen how sandwiches curl up at the edges when they're dry—well, *you* are'nt going to let that happen to yours. To wet the

napkin, just hold it under running water for a few seconds then squeeze it out well. Now its ready to use to keep your sandwiches juicy and moist, as they should be.

3. Another thing that you need to remember when you're setting out on a session of sandwich-making: keep the butter out of the fridge so it can soften. Of course, this is no problem in summer but if you think of it only at the last minute in winter, you will be battling the butter to make your sandwich filling!

4. Now to filling the sandwiches. The secret in this step is being generous. You want a nice, juicy sandwich not an uninteresting one that tastes more of bread than anything else. So fill it well and make sure you spread it out right to the edges. As you fill the sandwiches, once again, keep them covered with the wet napkin. Remove it, in fact, only when you're ready to serve.

5. After the sandwiches are all made, you will want to cut them—in triangles or rectangles. Remember how you cut the crusts? Go back and forth, pretending you're a carpenter, so all the filling that you've just put in doesn't come rushing angrily out. Smoothen and neaten the edges with a round-bladed knife.

6. To carry sandwiches on a picnic or to school, of course, you know how you can

keep them fresh—wrap them in foil or cling-film.

Should we make some then? I'm beginning to feel hungry just telling you all these 'rules'. Read on for some interesting ones.

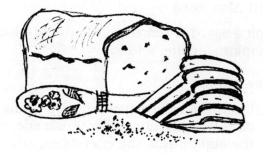

CHEESE AND CUCUMBER SANDWICHES

You Will Need For Four Sandwiches

4 slices bread

a small cucumber

4 teaspoons cheese spread*

2 teaspoons tomato sauce

a little bit of black pepper, if you like

a little bit of mustard, if you like

You Will Also Need

a chopping board, a sharp knife, a round-bladed knife, a wet napkin, a plate, a fork.

To Make Them

1. For these sandwiches, the first thing we must do is treat the cucumber. From one end, where the stalk meets the cucumber, cut off a little cap. With the sharp point of the knife, make a few lines in the cucumber. Maybe you can write the first letter of your name! Now take the cap you have cut off and start scrubbing the cucumber with it. A white froth will come out. Do it for a few minutes then cut off this little bit of the cucumber, and peel it. You know how to do that? With that punky vegetable peeler that I introduced you to earlier in the book. Once you've got all the skin off, wash the cucumber and cut it into thin slices. Yes, thin slices certainly are most suitable for

sandwiches. To do that, hold the cucumber on the board with your left hand and start slicing with your right. Keep moving your left hand back as you go along so you don't slice off a bit of your finger in the bargain. For these sandwiches, you will need just 8 slices. You can cover the rest of the cucumber with cling-film and put it back in the fridge to be used another time.

2. To make the filling, put the cheese spread, sauce, pepper and mustard, (if you're using them) on the plate and with a fork, mix them up well. Take a little lick to see if it tastes fine, or you need to add something more.

3. You did read the introduction to this chapter, didn't you? So you know how to make good sandwiches? Now let's see you making these— cut the crusts off, then spread the cheese filling on all 4 slices. Put 4 cucumber slices on 2 slices and cover with the other two. Press down gently and then cut, neatly so you get two cucumber slices in each sandwich. Well done!

4. Keep covered with a wet napkin if you're not eating them immediately.

*So what if you don't have cheese spread at home—make your own. Put 2 teaspoons of butter on your plate, grate some tinned cheese (about 1/2 cup) onto it, add the sauce, pepper and mustard and mash it all together to make a delicious spread. Of course, you'll remember to use the grater for the cheese, won't you?

31

EGG SANDWICHES

You Will Need For Four Sandwiches

4 slices bread   a large pinch of salt
1 egg   a small pinch of black pepper
3-4 teaspoons butter   mustard, if you like
1 tablespoon tomato sauce

You Will Also Need

a chopping board, a sharp knife, a round-blade knife, a wet napkin, a plate, a fork and a small pan preferably with a lid and handle, oven-gloves, a large spoon.

To Make Them

1. Let's boil the egg. To do this, put it in the small handled pan. Add enough water to just cover it. Put the lid on and set the pan on the fire. Ask an adult to help you light the gas, if needed. The water will start boiling, in a few minutes (you will be able to hear the egg gently murmuring!). Turn down the heat and leave the pan on the fire for 5 minutes.

2. Wearing your oven gloves, take the lid off. (Don't stick your face over the pan unless you want to steam it!) With the spoon, carefully take the egg out and put it on a plate or the counter top to cool. As soon as you can easily handle it, peel it and put it it on a plate. Cut it up into half. Add all the other things—3 teaspoons of the butter, sauce, salt, pepper, mustard. Mash it all well together with a fork. You should not have bits of egg

32

in the spread—it should be almost creamy. If it isn't, you can add the extra teaspoon of butter. Taste a little and see if you need to add anything more. If not, just go ahead and make the sandwiches. We discussed that already, didn't we?

3. Keep them covered with the wet napkin if you're not eating them immediately.

4. By the way, a few teaspoons of cheese spread added to this mixture tastes delicious. Try it some time.

SALAMI OR HAM SANDWICHES

You Will Need For Four Sandwiches

4 slices bread

4 teaspoons butter

a few drops of lemon juice

3 teaspoons tomato sauce

a dot of mustard, if you like

a pinch of pepper

2 leaves of lettuce, nicely washed (if it's in season)

8 slices of salami or 2 slices of ham

You Will Also Need

a chopping board, a sharp knife, a round-bladed knife, a wet napkin, a plate, a fork.

To Make Them

1. Put the butter, lemon juice, tomato sauce, mustard, if you're using it and the pepper on the plate. Mix and mash it together well with the fork. Spread it neatly over each slice of bread. (Of course, you would have cut the crusts off). On two of the slices, put 4 slices each of salami or of ham. If the salami is too big, cut it in half and use just two slices on each slice of bread. Top with the other buttered slice.
2. Cut the sandwiches neatly. Specially in the case of ham or salami, you would be wise to remember how to cut the bread like a carpenter.
3. Keep them covered with the wet napkin if you're not eating them immediately.

JAM SANDWICHES

You Will Need For Four Sandwiches

4 slices bread
some butter
some jam

You Will Also Need

a chopping board, a sharp knife, a round-bladed knife, a wet napkin, a plate.

To Make Them

1. Cut the crusts off the bread, as you are now expert at doing.
2. Spread butter on each of the slices. I haven't mentioned how much butter so you can go ahead and be greedy and use as much as you like. Do the same with the jam. Spread it out neatly right to the edges. Top with one of the buttered slices, press it together gently and put it under the wet napkin. I beg your pardon— you're planning to eat it right away?. O.K., just go ahead then!
3. I know these jam sandwiches must be one of your favourites but tell me, have you ever tried jam and cheese sandwiches? Yes, I did say cheese, you're not hearing wrong! If you haven't tried them, please just take my word for it—add a slice of cheese over the jam or on one of the slices, instead of butter, use cheese spread. Bite into it now—aren't the sweet and salty flavours just so perfect together?

35

SAUCE SANDWICHES

When you feel like having one of these sandwiches, do you often hear remarks like this:
"What sort of sandwich is that?"
"Are you sure you want **just** sauce in it? Wouldn't you like some cheese too?"
Well, learn to make them for yourself and you won't have to find answers to those questions!

You Will Need For Four Sandwiches

4 slices bread
some butter
some sauce

You Will Also Need

a chopping board, a sharp knife, a round-bladed knife, a plate.

To Make Them

1. Cut the crusts off the bread. I'm sure you can do that so well now.
2. Butter each slice of bread well, right to the edges. This is the secret here—the butter will stop the sauce from soaking through and making the sandwiches soggy.
3. Pour on the sauce—some on each slice. Spread it out evenly and cover with the second slice.
4. Cut in triangles or rectangles.
5. Eat! If you're not planning to, cover it with a wet napkin. Yes, I agree, you don't need cheese or anything else but perhaps, you might consider experimenting with different sauces or a sprinkle of pepper over the sauce for a spicy change.

36

CARROT SPREAD SANDWICHES

These sandwiches are so different and so delicious. You have to try them when carrots are in season.

You Will Need For Four Sandwiches

4 slices bread	1/2 cube of cheese (if you
1 small carrot	have it at home)
4 teaspoons butter	1/4 teaspoon salt
a few drops of lemon juice	1/4 teaspoon pepper

You Will Also Need

a chopping board, a sharp knife, a round-bladed knife, a plate, a fork, a vegetable peeler, a grater.

To Make Them

1. Wash and peel the carrot. Use the vegetable peeler to do it. Wash it again.
2. Using the grater, grate the carrot into the plate.
3. To the carrot, add the butter, salt, pepper, lemon juice and cheese, if you're using it. Mash and mix it all together well with the fork. Taste to see if you need anything more. The spread should be creamy, not dry so add some more butter if it is needed.
4. Make the sandwiches as we discussed earlier—cut the crusts off the bread and spread each slice with some of the delicious spread you've made, pair up the slices and cut them into rectangles or triangles.

37

Note: You can keep this spread in the fridge if it's left-over, to enjoy it another day. In fact, why not just make a cupful of it whenever you're in the mood and then you'll have an instant spread for your toast.

Now, we've talked about quite a few fillings. How about taking a peep into the fridge to see what leftovers we could also use for sandwiches?
What if you spy

LEFT-OVER *SOOKHA ALU* (COOKED DRY POTATOES)

You have the makings of an interesting sandwich. For each sandwich, mash 1 slightly heaped tablespoon of the vegetable with a little butter and some tomato sauce. Taste—stop eating it all up now, you've forgotten we were making sandwich fillings!

LEFT-OVER *KEEMA* (MINCE)

You're in luck. Do what you did to the potatoes and you have a really satisfying sandwich, perhaps even a meal!

LEFT-OVER *RAJMAH* (KIDNEY BEANS)

Yes, that's right. Just pick out the beans with just a little gravy—just as much as you need to mash them to a smooth spread. Add a few teapoons butter and if you like chillies, some chopped up green chillies. You're ready to taste now and then fill.

LEFT-OVER CHICKEN OR MEAT:

Lucky again! Look closer to see if there isn't by any chance, some mayonnaise lying around. There is? You're in for a treat! Put 2 pieces of chicken or 3-4 pices of meat on to a plate. With your fingers, pull the meat off the bone. Mix with the mayonnaise or some butter, add some tomato sauce if you like it and you're ready to make some delicious sandwiches.

39

Now I can see your minds really ticking. Yes, you can use any left-overs provided they are dry-cooked. With a little imagination, you can use them to make delightfully different sandwiches.

But perhaps you don't always want to have them cold. You feel like having a warmed up snack. Well, then you can make **TOASTED SANDWICHES**. See the gadget drawn on the next page? You might have one like it at home. You do? Well, then all you have to do is make a sandwich—any of them that we talked about—and put it into the 'toaster'. The neatest way of doing it is this:

1. Open up the gadget and lay it flat on the counter top.
2. Drop half a teaspoonful of butter on each side. With your finger, rub it all over well.
3. Carefully put your sandwich on one side, then close the gadget over it.
4. Close the hook to hold it shut.
5. Put on the gas. Ask for help to do this, if you need. Holding it by the end of its handle, hold the toaster over the flame for about 3 minutes.
6. Turn over and do the same the other side.
7. Lay it on the counter top, open the hook, and with oven gloves on, lift up one side gently to see that it's toasted as you like it.
8. If it still needs cooking, repeat the process for another few minutes on each side.

9. Take it out gently—you may need to use a knife to ease the edges wherever they've stuck slightly.

Put your sandwich on a plate, get yourself a napkin and you're ready to eat.

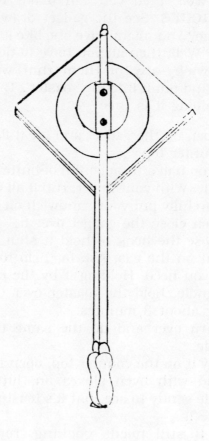

GRILLED SANDWICHES

H ere're some more sandwiches for your hungry moments, kids. These are grilled and called open sandwiches—that means they have only one slice of bread, with a spread of course—but no second slice covering it.

You Will Need for FOUR Grilled Cheese Sandwiches

4 slices bread	a little black pepper
2 teaspoons butter	1 green chilli, if you like,
$1/2$ cup grated cheese	OR
2 tablespons tomato sauce	a small capsicum. if in season

You Will Also Need

a chopping board, a sharp knife, a round-bladed knife, a plate, a fork, an oven-tray, oven-gloves, a timer.

To Make Them

1. Put the grill in your oven on. Ask an adult for help if you need.
2. Cut the crusts off the bread using the sharp knife. Keep the slices covered.
3. Chop the chilli or capsicum. If you're using the chilli, wash it and lay it on your cutting board. Hold it with your left hand and then close to it, cut it thinly along its length, moving your left hand back as you go along. You will

43

cut the capsicum the same way but as you will not be using the whole of it, just cut out a slice from the capsicum. Cut up in little bits, as tiny as you can make them.

4. Mix together all the things, except the bread. Taste and see if the spread needs anything to be added to it. If it tastes good, spread it onto the slices, using an equal amount for each.

5. Put the slices of bread onto the oven tray and wearing your oven gloves, put it into the oven. Wait 4–5 minutes, as patiently as possible. You can use the timer now. When the cheesey smell makes it unbearable to control yourself any longer, take a peek. The toasts should be done which means nicely browned on the top. Take them out, again wearing your gloves, of course. You needn't wait a minute longer now!

Capsicum, Cheese, Mouse eatings

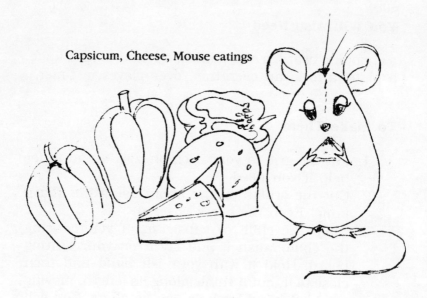

GRILLED CHEESE AND TOMATO SANDWICHES

Make the cheese spread as in the last recipe. Spread it onto the slices of bread but before putting it into the oven, lay two slices of tomato on each. Grate some more cheese on top before grilling.

GRILLED HAM SANDWICHES

Make the cheese spread as in the recipe for Grilled Cheese Sandwiches. If you don't want to use cheese, make a butter spread, like you did for the Sauce Sandwich. Spread onto the bread. Lay the ham on top, and on it put a slice of tomato. You can even slice some strips of capsicum and lay them in a pretty criss-cross design. Do you know what I mean? Yes, make multiplication signs all over or addition ones if you prefer! Grill the sandwich, as you did for the earlier ones.
Of course, instead of ham, you can use salami.

Similarly, you can make grilled sandwiches with almost any filling—the meat and chicken spreads that we talked about would do very well. But what makes these grilled ones special is if you grate cheese over because it melts so temptingly when the sandwich is done.

PICTURE SANDWICHES

Well, children, until now, we've only been talking of normal sandwiches—delicious but normal. Now we're going to have some REAL fun dressing those very ones up. Let's suppose you have some friends coming over for tea or perhaps even your grand-parents and you want to treat them to some really surprising sandwiches. Well, that's exactly how these will look when you're done with them.

You know what I call them? PICTURE SANDWICHES.

Before you start to make the sandwiches—you can make any of the ones we've talked about—you have to decide which shape you're going to try out first. Here are lots of ideas—try them all.

You will need steel *katoris* (bowls) as well as bottle tops of different sizes to cut the bread.

You will also need some butter to 'stick on' the decorations.

FACE-ON-A-PLATE SANDWICHES

To make these you need to cut **two** slices of white or brown bread round.

1. Take a steel *katori* (bowl) as close to the size of the slice of bread as possible. Upturn the bowl on the bread and press down.
2. Tear away all the extra bits from the side.
3. Do the same with another slice of bread. You will need to cut two circles for each sandwich.
4. Now go ahead and make the spread of your chcice and fill it in.

46

5. Now let's make a face on the upper slice—take two small slices of anything round—cucumber, radish (*mooli*), carrot for the eyes. Add a pepper-corn for the pupils. You could even use two sweet gems.
6. Put anything straight—a chilly, chip-sticks—for the nose.
7. Use half a slice of tomato for a smiling red mouth and your sandwich has actually come alive!
8. Now make it into a girl if you like. Give her some curly hair made of grated cheese and a necklace and earrings made of small sweets or more gems. If you prefer a boy, give him straight chip-sticks hair and no ear-rings or necklace.
9. Serve it on a pretty plate.

HOUSE-ON-A-PLATE
SANDWICHES

Here's another super idea!

1. Cut 1 **slice of bread** in half to get two rectangles and **another** to get two triangles.

House on a Plate Sandwich

2. Fill the sandwiches.

3. Put one rectangle on your plate for the main house and the triangle on top for the roof. Doesn't that look like the house you used to draw when you were in Nursery?

4. Now give it a door, cut out of a slice of carrot or you could use a bit of tomato or cucumber.

5. Add a window too and a chimney if you want.

6. For a really lived in look, lets have some smoke coming out of the chimney too—some Crax rings might come in handy here or maybe just a few ordinary chips.

7. And how about some grass—use any greens torn up finely—cabbage, spinach, coriander (*dhaniya*).

8. Or perhaps, instead of the grass, your house could have a path of baked beans! Come on, be really imaginative.

HEDGEHOG-ON-A-PLATE SANDWICHES

Yes, you're going to make and eat a hedgehog now. If you like brown bread, definitely make him out of it.

1. Again, you need to cut **1 slice of bread** in a circle as you did for the face.
2. Now cut it again in half so you get two semi-circles.
3. Fill and stick them together and put on a plate. Now lets give your hedgehog some life.
4. Add a beady, black, pepper-corn eye.
5. Let's have some chip-sticks sticking out all over his body, stuck with dots of butter.
6. Put a dot of tomato sauce for a red nose. Excellent!
7. Is he sitting on grass—use the greens as in the last recipe or let him lie on a bed of baked beans perhaps, if he prefers sniffing around among stones!

RABBIT-ON-A-PLATE SANDWICHES

This one is just too charming to eat but you can try!

1. Cut **two slices of bread in circles,** as for the face. Out of **another two slices** cut two smaller circles, with the help of a smaller steel bowl.
2. When you've made the sandwiches, first put the big circle on the plate. Position the smaller one as you can see in the picture.

3. Cut out the ears—try a green-leaf like spinach or cabbage—you can use a clean scissor to cut out the shape and stick them in place with a dab of butter.

4. Eyes? Nothing like it if it's the season for pomegranates (*anaar*). Then you can have truly realistic, pink eyes otherwise use pepper corns.

5. Add the mouth—sauce is the easiest to 'draw with'.

6. And don't forget the whiskers—uncooked noodles will do just fine or chip-sticks, if you want eatable ones.

7. For the final touch, how about some popcorn for his little tail? Add some grass again if you like made of chopped cabbage. Now wasn't I right? Isn't he too charming to eat?

TOADSTOOL-ON-A-PLATE SANDWICHES

Of course, by now **you** can tell me how to make a toadstool!

1. Yes, cut **1 slice of boread** in half to get 2 rectangles and **another slice** in semi-circles. Make them into sandwiches.
2. Position them to make the toadstool.
3. Certainly, give it some green around it and then some pop-corn spots, or even ones made out of gems for a really colourful effect.
4. And don't forget you can use brown and white breads to effect too. Brown toadstools with white dots, for example. You can cut the dots out easily, using any bottle-top.

FLOWER-ON-A-PLATE SANDWICHES

Well, what could we think of after toad-stools other than flowers? Actually, this one is a flower in a pot.

1. Cut **one slice of bread** into 2 triangles or semicircles and **another slice of bread** into two small circles. Any small steel bowl or biscuit cutter will help you do it.
2. Make the sandwiches—one a triangle, the other a small circle.
3. Put the pot (thats the triangle or semi-circle) onto your plate. Now first lets have a nice green stem—a chilly or bean sticking out of it.
4. Now for the flower. Put your circle on the top of the stem—that's the centre of the flower—and put chips all around.
5. Stick them into the sandwich, between the two slices. Of course, they will get a little soggy by the time you eat them but I'm sure your friends will be too delighted to mind.
6. Now the finishing touches: you can decorate the centre of the flower: stick on some crushed chips. You can even grate some cheese or put dots of tomato sauce all over.
7. Like to add some leaves? Cut them out of lettuce or spinach and position them on both sides of the stem. Do you like the effect? I'm sure you do.

Those were some ideas for single servings. Now how about presenting sandwiches for a group? All together? Heres something you can do.

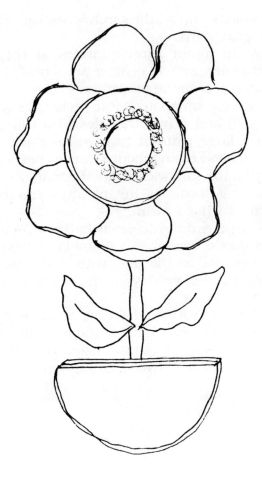

THE SANDWICH HOUSE

1. First make up all the sandwiches you will need for your party.
2. Cut up about three-quarters of them into rectangles and a quarter into triangles. For example, if you've made twelve sandwiches (24 slices) cut up about 8 into rectangles (you will get 16) and 4 into triangles (you will get 8)
3. On a large plate or tray, make stacks of the rectangles keeping about 4 sandwiches per stack.
4. Across the sandwiches, lay the triangles to form the roof. Look at the picture—you will see exactly what I mean.
5. Now go ahead and decorate the house. Remember the doors, windows, a chimney. I have stuck chip-sticks on the roof, with butter for a nice rural effect or you try wafers for a more modern one.
6. Of course, you need greens all around and if you have some small plastic animals or dolls, let them roam around outside your house for a really imaginative finishing touch.

The Sandwich House

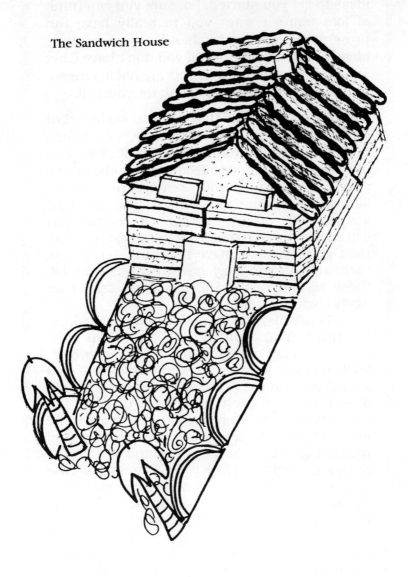

Well, kids, I think I've given you quite a few ideas to get you started. I'm sure you can think of lots more. I want you to really have fun presenting these sandwiches. Use some of these ideas but don't get upset if you don't have Crax at home for example or carrots are not in season. Improvise, which means think for yourself.

Use other things that you can easily get at home. Just peep into the fridge or kitchen cupboard and I am sure you will discover lots of things you can use effectively. Another thing you can do to make really interesting sandwiches is cut the bread into different shapes with biscuit cutters. Of course, you will remember to cut at least two of each shape, then go ahead and have real fun   dressing them up. As you may have realised yourself, these sandwiches would look best served on plain coloured plates.

There's just one thing that you have to keep in mind. You remember I told you how sandwiches dry out if they're left out, uncovered. Well, that's a problem. It would be best if you kept them arranged in their plates, covered with a wet napkin each and then put on the decorations just before eating. You need to be extra organised—keep every thing ready and together and then just dash in and put on the finishing touches before you serve. In the case of the big house (the last recipe) you can stack the sandwiches, even decorate the house and keep it covered with a big napkin.

Another thing that you would do well to remember is that some of the pictures need more than one sandwich to make them—the rabbit, the house, the flower for example. I'm sure most of you have no problem gobbling up two sandwiches but in case you have a younger guest who can't, make a smaller picture or choose one which needs just one sandwich—a small face, or a hedgehog for example, so that no food is wasted.

Talking about wastage, unfortunately, you do have some scraps of bread leftover from the sides after you've cut out circles. While you're still working, you can keep them to cut out smaller eyes or other such things you need for your pictures. When you're finished, however, maybe you'd like to give the birds a party too. Throw them all the crumbs!

There are also some decorations that I don't expect you to eat—uncooked noodles, foil, pepper—throw them away when your party is over.

But the fun's not over yet—look, there're still more sandwiches coming your way!

RIBBON SANDWICHES

Tell me, have you eaten ribbon sandwiches? They're exciting and so easy to make. Want to try?

1. First, you need three or four different fillings. Choose them and make them.
2. Then take three slices of bread (if you have two fillings) and four, if you have three.
3. Cut off the crusts.
4. Put the first filling between two slices. Put the second filling onto another slice and stick it, filling side down onto the first two slices. Do the same with the last slice and last filling.
5. Now you have four slices sitting on top of each other. Carefully, like a carpenter, sawing back and forth, cut the sandwiches into thick strips. You should get three or four.
6 Arrange them on a plate as you keep cutting. Don't they look pretty with their different ribbons of colour?
7. Keep them covered till you eat and remember to choose fillings that taste good with each other—cheese and sauce and cucumber for example or meat and chutney and sauce or— there are so many, each more delicious than the other.

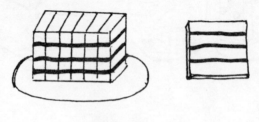

FASHIONABLE SANDWICHES

Here's one more thing you can do to really make fashion-conscious sandwiches. You know how black and white is in fashion in clothes? Well, brown and white is 'in' as far as sandwiches go.

To make these sandwiches, here is what you do

1. First of all, you need both brown and white bread, and you need to do some calculations before you start. Decide how many sandwiches you want at the end and take out that same number of slices, both brown and white, approximately half of each.

BROWN AND WHITE CIRCLES

1. Lets have a base of white. With a steel bowl as close to the size of the slice of bread as possible, cut out a circle.
2. Spread with whichever filling you've chosen.
3. Cover the sandwich with one semi-circle of white and one of brown. Isn't that attractive ?

WHEELS WITHIN WHEELS

1. Cut out one circle of brown.
2. Spread with filling.
3. Cut out yet another circle of the same size in white bread.
4. From the centre of the white circle, cut out with a smaller bowl or bottle-top, another circle.
5. Take another slice of brown bread. Cut it into a circle and from its center, cut out the smaller circle.

6. Fit this smaller brown circle into the space on the white circle and use the smaller white one to fill the gap in the brown.

Sounds confusing? It isn't—not when you do it and certainly not for clever kids like you.

BROWN AND WHITE CHECKS

1. Cut off the crusts from one slice of white bread.
2. Spread with filling.
3. Cut another slice into rectangles and then again in half to get four squares. Do the same to a slice of brown bread.
4. Top the filling with one check in brown, the next in white, another brown one next to the white and white next to the brown. Looks like a game-board doesn't it?

Now, children, you think up some more combinations In fact, have a party designing these super sandwiches. Just remember though, that since each sandwich uses almost two slices of bread each, they are big so cater accordingly. By the way, don't forget you can make ribbon sandwiches too, using alternating slices of brown and white. Have fun!

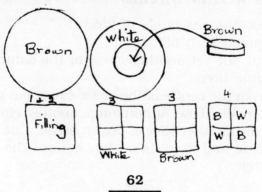

FAVOURITE DRINKS

Here are some really useful recipes for drinks I know you enjoy. Learn to make them yourself and then you don't have to depend on an adult to do it for you. So next time, any of you feel like having a cold glass of *nimbu pani* or a tall, filling milk-shake or cold coffee, just open your book, follow the recipe and you should soon be sipping something delicious. In fact, it's just what you need to make for yourself with one of the sandwiches in the last section.

Of course, for most of these, you need a blender so before you decide to ask for permission to borrow it, you better be on your best behaviour: listen attentively to all instructions about what you can and cannot do to it and restate your promise to clean it up perfectly after you've finished. If you make up one of these refreshing drinks for the adults in your family too, I'm sure you'll always get the permission easily in the future too!

By the way, the last recipe in this section is a little surprise for you from me. I hope you enjoy it.

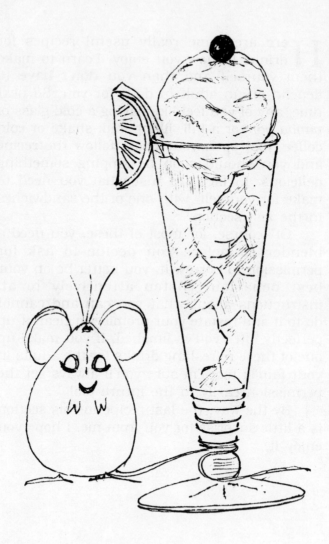

NIMBU PANI

(Fresh Lime Water)

You Will Need for ONE Glass

3-4 teaspoons sugar   water
$^1/_2$ lemon   ice, if needed

You Will Also Need

a lemon squeezer, a spoon, a glass

To Make It

1. Put the sugar and a few tablespoons of water into the glass. Stir it briskly till the sugar is dissolved. That means you should not be able to see the little grains rushing around at the bottom of the glass.
2. Now you can squeeze the lemon into the water. The lemon squeezer we met earlier can help you.
3. Add 1-2 ice-cubes if you want your drink really cold otherwise just fill the glass up with cold water and stir well.

INSTANT NIMBU PANI

(Fresh Lime Water)

Here's something useful you can do that I'm sure everyone in your family will love you for. Can you imagine the joy of a *nimbu-pani* without any last minute stirring and squeezing? Just make this mixture, keep it in a bottle in the fridge and help yourself to it anytime you need.

You Will Need for ONE Bottle

12 lemons
2 cups sugar

1 cup water

You Will Also Need :

2 pans, one larger than the other, a long spoon to stir with, a clean hanky, a plastic strainer, an empty bottle— the kind you get squashes in, a funnel or jug with a spout

To Make It

1. Cut the lemons in half and squeeze out the juice, into the smaller pan. Use the lemon squeeze to do it.
2. Into the second pan, put the sugar and the water. Put it onto a slow fire and stir every once in a while till the sugar melts. You should not be able to see any grains of it on your stirring spoon. Raise the heat to high and let the sugar come to a boil. Be careful—it will bubble up as it boils. Put the fire off.

66

3. Pour the lemon juice into the sugar syrup and stir well. Leave it to cool for about 15 minutes.

4. Over the first pan, fix or hold the strainer. Lay the hanky in the bowl of the strainer too. If you're holding the strainer because it isn't one of those big ones that can rest on the rim of your pan, ask someone else to pour the syrup through it. Shake with the spoon if you find it is not going through fast enough. Watch out! It might spill out of the bowl. Take another if you need.

5. When it has cooled fully, pour into a bottle and keep in the fridge. The neatest way of doing this is to pour it through a clean plastic funnel or a jug or glass with a small spout.

6. To make yourself a glass of instant *nimbu-pani*, just pour a few tablespoons of the ready-made mixture into a glass and fill up with water and ice-cubes. Stir well before you drink.

Shall I give you another bright idea? Do you like mint? That's *pudina*, by the way. If you do, wash a leaf of it well, tear it up into little pieces and mix into your *nimbu-pani*. If you don't like it too much yourself, at least remember to offer it to your guests and do it in style: What will you have? you can ask. Would you like your *nimbu-pani* plain or with mint ?!

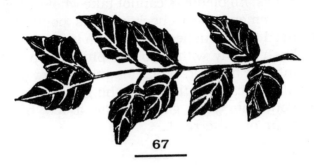

MANY FLAVOURED MILK SHAKES

Now we're going to make another of your favourites—
Milk Shakes. I've seen you slurping these up in ice-
cream parlours. Now how about making some
yourself?

Mango Milk Shake
You Will Need for ONE Tall Glass

1 large slice of mango   1-2 teaspoons of sugar
or 2 small ones   1-2 ice-cubes
1 glass of milk

You Will Also Need:

a spoon, a blender, a glass, a straw, if you think you need it

To Make It

1. Scoop out the mango from the shell with the
   spoon, just as you do when you're eating it.
   Drop it into the blender. Cap the blender
   carefully and whizz it for a few seconds.
2. Open the cap, pour in the sugar, milk and ice-
   cubes. All blenders cannot take whole ice-cubes
   so remember to check on this point. If they
   need to be crushed, wrap them in a napkin and
   bash lightly with a rolling pin then put them
   into the blender. Whizz for another few seconds
   till you can see that everything is nicely mixed.
3. Pour into your glass. Drink a few big sips.
   Pour out the rest!

MANGO MILK-SHAKE WITH ICE-CREAM

Buy a small cup of vanilla or mango ice-cream. Carefully scoop it out and put into your glass of mango milk shake. Put a straw in it if you like, and also, give yourself a spoon to eat the ice-cream.

BANANA MILK-SHAKE

Make it exactly like the mango one, except that instead of the mango, use one small banana. You can top it with the vanilla ice-cream too, if you like.

CHOCOLATE MILK-SHAKE

Put one glass of milk, 1-2 teaspoons of sugar, and 1 teaspoon cocoa or drinking chocolate into the blender. For a richer chocolate flavour, add an extra spoonful. Whizz up in the blender. Of course, you can add the scoop of vanilla ice-cream or may be a chocolate one to top up this already delicious drink to make it a dream come true!

STRAWBERRY MILK-SHAKE

This is only for those lucky ones among you who live in a place where you can get fresh strawberries. Well, when you do, remember to make this for yourself. Instead of the mango in the mango milk-shake, use $1/2$ cupful of strawberries. Wash them well, cut them in half and drop them into the blender. Add the rest of the ingredients as for the other milk-shakes. How I wish I lived where you do. We never get to see decent strawberries in Delhi.

69

COLD COFFEE

You Will Need for ONE Glass

1 glass of milk	$1/2$ —1 teaspoon coffee*
1 teaspoon of any malted	$1^1/_2$—2 teaspoons sugar*
chocolate	ice-cubes, if needed

You Will Also Need

a blender, a small pan, a spoon

To Make It

1. Put the malted chocolate, coffee and sugar into the glass.
2. Heat a few tablespoons of milk in the pan. Pour it over the coffee and sugar in the glass. Stir to dissolve well. This is the secret of good cold-coffee.
3. Now put the coffee mixture into the blender with the milk and ice, if you're using it. Whizz up and drink instantly. The delicious fragrance won't let you wait in any case!

Note: You will see little stars against the coffee and sugar. Let me explain why they are there. I have written 1/2-1 teaspoon coffee because I think $1/2$ teaspoon should be quite enough for you but an adult in your family may need more—upto one teaspoon. The same goes for the sugar. Put in $1^1/_2$-2 teaspoons, depending on how sweet you like your drink. I hope you won't need more than 2 teaspoons but of course, its possible!

71

To make cold coffee with ice-cream:

Yes, by now, you know what to do. Get yourself a small cup of vanilla ice-cream and drop it into your glass of frothy cold coffee, fresh from the blender.

Blender, Coffee, Ice Milk

LASSI*

Do you like *lassi*? I do, though I like the salted one and I can bet you prefer the sweet one. Want to make yourself a glass?

You Will Need for ONE Glass

$^1/_2$ cup of *dahi* (curd) if you want a thinnish *lassi* and a little more if you prefer it thicker

$^1/_2$ cup of water
1-2 ice-cubes, if needed

$^1/_4$ teaspoon of salt and a little less of pepper
or
3-4 teaspoons sugar

You Will Also Need

a blender, a glass

To Make It

1. Put all the things you need for the *lassi* into the blender.
2. Add the salt and pepper if you want salty *Lassi* and the sugar if you prefer to have it sweet,
3. Whizz for a few seconds. Pour into a glass and it's ready to drink.

---

*a drink made from curds.

SPICY COLA

Here's something I know you'll get addicted to. Do you know what that means? That means you will begin enjoying it so much you will drink it in quantities that are not good for you! Now, don't do that but enjoy it once in a while.

You Will Need for ONE Glass

any cola drink   a pinch of *kala namak* or *Chaat masala*
$^1/_2$ lemon

You Will Also Need :

a glass, a spoon, a bottle opener, a lemon squeezer

To Make It

1. Open the bottle of drink. Pour into the glass.
2. Squeeze in a few drops from the lemon—about half of the half—and also add the *masala.*
3. Stir well. As you do that, your drink will fizz up. Make sure it doesn't fall out of the glass.
4. Take a sip. See if you need a little more lemon or *masala.* No? Then just enjoy it. Doesn't it taste like something you might get used to having?

74

MELON COOLER

Can you imagine two favourites together—watermelon and ice-cream? That's exactly what this drink is all about—you just have to try it.

You Will Need, for ONE Glass

$^1/_2$ cup chopped watermelon pieces
1 small cup vanilla ice-cream

a few tablespoons milk
1-2 teaspoons sugar
ice-cubes, if needed

You Will Also Need

a blender, a glass

To Make It

1. Put the fruit, ice and the ice-cream into the blender. Add a few tablespoons milk—you can add more if you find your drink is too thick for your liking. Also, start by adding 1 teaspoon sugar, whizz, taste and add more later if needed. The amount you add may differ each time you make it, depending on the sweetness of the melon. Whizz for a few seconds. Add more milk if needed, before pouring out.

FLAVOURED ICE-CUBES

If it's summer, there's no better way to beat the heat than sucking on one of these or perhaps I should say, some of these?!

You Will Need for ONE Ice-Tray Full

$^1/_2$ cup of your favourite squash

$1^1/_2$ cups of water

some wooden ice-cream spoons

You Will Also Need:

a jug or bowl, a spoon, a measuring cup, an ice-tray, preferably a plastic one

To Make It

1. Measure the squash and water into the jug or bowl. Mix with the spoon. Taste. It should taste much sweeter than you normally have it. Add more water, if needed.
2. Pour it into the tray. Put it into the freezer.
3. Check on it after 2-3 hours. If it is beginning to set, stick one ice-cream spoon, the fatter side down, into each cube. Put back in the freezer to allow it to set fully.
4. Whenever you want a cooling lick, take out the tray and twist one cube out. It is better to make this recipe in the evening and put it

away for the night so that you don't keep waiting and drooling while the cubes are setting.

Note: You can also set these in moulds made specially for ice-lollys. They look like the bars of ice-cream you buy. You will have to calculate the quantities depending on the size. Make this amount and then some more if you need. Also, I can tell you another way of doing this that your mother might hate me for but I'll take the risk. Instead of squash, use any aerated drink. Pour it straight into the tray and freeze.

SNACKS FOR ALL TIMES

I bet this is going to be one of your favourite chapters—and the one that you will use most often, for isn't it always snack-time? Especially when the snacks mean delicious spicy, sour-sweet *Chaats*, crisp *tikkis*, cheesy pizzas and... I won't make your mouths water any more now. Just turn the page, select whatever you most feel like eating—let me warn you the choice is a little difficult—and lets get started. Whether you've just come back from school, or whether you feel like eating something with your glass of milk or whether it's that in-between time between meals and you feel like munching something, go ahead. And don't cook only for yourself—these are all snacks that are so much more enjoyable if you have friends and family to share them with. None are difficult to make but some of them do require preparation: for example, if you want to make a pizza, you have to get the pizza bases, if you want to make the *Channa Chaat*, you must soak the *channas* at least a couple of hours before they can be boiled, for the *Papri Chaat* you need to get the *papris* and so on. So read the recipes and get your act together before you get too hungry and just can't wait any longer!

First, all the *Chaats*. Even the younger ones among you can assemble them without any problem but since you need to use the pressure cooker in come cases, please ask on adult or older brother or sister to help.

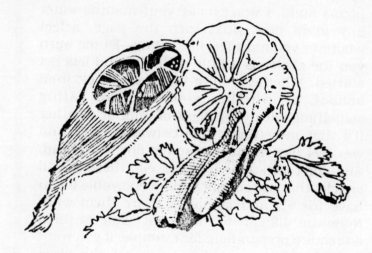

CHATPATA CHANNA CHAAT
(A Chickpea Snack)

You Will Need for FOUR People

$^1/_2$ cup chick-pease (*Safed channe*)
2 potatoes, washed well
2 tomatoes, washed well
2 lemons

about $^1/_2$ teaspoon of salt
a pinch of black salt
2 teaspoons sugar
2 teaspoons *chaat masala*
2-3 teaspoons water

You Will Also Need:

a pressure cooker, a lemon squeezer, teaspoons, a cup, a bowl, a knife, a chopping board.

To Make It

1. Put the chickpease in a bowl and wash well. To do that, pour some water over, rub them well, drain the water and then repeat 3-4 times. Finally, pour $1^1/_2$ cups clean drinking water over them and leave them to soak in it overnight or for at least 3 hours.
2. When you want to cook, put the *channas* with the water in which they were soaked into the pressure cooker. Close the cooker and put it on the fire. After it whistles, turn down the heat and keep on the fire for 10 minutes. Put off the fire and after 15 minutes, open the cooker. Test to check if they're done by squeezing one of them (you can keep the water

81

aside and ask your parents if they would like to use it in some *dal* that is being cooked that day).

3. Now you have to boil the potatoes. Put them also into the cooker with 1 cup of water. After the cooker whistles, turn down the heat and keep it on the fire for 5 minutes. Take off the fire and open the cooker after about 10 minutes. Take the potatoes out and keep aside. Both the chick-pease and potatoes should be boiled in advance because in any case, you need both things to be cool for the *chaat*. In case you are in the age-group that is not allowed to light the fire yourself, ask an adult to help you with these steps. The rest you should be able to do quite easily.

4. When the potatoes are cool, peel them and chop into pieces, as big or as small as you like.

5. Cut the tomatoes in 4-6 pieces each. You read about how to do that in the first few pages, didn't you? Add them, along with the potatoes to the *channas* in the bowl.

6. Over the *channas*, potatoes, and tomatoes, squeeze the juice of the lemons. You can use your lemon squeezer to do this and remember to pick out any seeds that might fall in.

7. Into the same bowl, sprinkle the salts.

8. Dissolve the sugar in the water by mixing well. Add the *chaat masala* and mix it in well too. Pour into the bowl.

8. Mix everything, gently without mashing the *channas* or breaking the potatoes. Take a test-bite and see if you need to add anything else. If not, stop eating and offer everyone else first!

By the way, how do you like the title of this recipe? Quite a tongue twister, isn't it? Challenge your friends to repeat it—fast!

ALU CHAAT

(Spicy Potato Snack)

Isn't this what all of us just can't resist? Its so very simple to make too. I know you're going to enjoy doing it.

You Will Need for FOUR People

4 large potatoes   1-2 teaspoons *chaat masala*
1 lemon   green chillies, if you like

You Will Also Need

a pressure cooker, a lemon squeezer, a teaspoon, a knife, a chopping board, a serving bowl

To Make It

1. First, you have to boil the potatoes. If you look at the recipe for *Channa Chaat*, you will know just how to do it. For *Chaat*, it is best to do it at least a couple of hours before you need to use them. Not only do they then have a chance to cool but it is less messy to cut and peel cooled potatoes. If you try to handle hot ones, you will more likely than not get crumbly, irregular pieces. So, keep them away till they're cool then gently peel them and cut them into neat pieces.
2. Put them into a serving bowl. Squeeze the juice of the lemon over. Also add the *chaat masala*—

start by adding one teaspoon then mix in gently, taste and decide if you need some more. More likely than not, you will not need to add salt but in case you feel you do, add a little. Also sprinkle in the green chillies if you're using them. Naturally, you would wash and chop them finely before doing it

3. Put the *chaat* in the fridge to cool till you need it. Just before serving, mix it well.

Note: I think this quantity should serve 4 but if it's as good as I think it's going to be maybe even 3 of you can polish it off without any problem!

Lemon, Potatoes, Green Chillis, Serving Bowl

FUN-COOKING FOR CHILDREN

FRUIT CHAAT

Is your mouth watering just reading this recipe? Go on, make some for yourself—it's good for you too.

You Will Need for TWO People

2 bananas	2 teaspoons *chaat masala*
2 guavas	A pinch of red chilli powder,
1 large-apple	if you like
2 lemons	$^1/_4$ teaspoon salt

$^1/_4$ teaspoon black salt, if you like

You Will Also Need

a knife, a potato peeler, a lemon squeezer, a bowl, a chopping board, a tablespoon

To Make It

1. Peel the banana. On the chopping board, chop it into thin slices and put it into the bowl. Immediately squeeze the juice of 1 lemon over it. Use the lemon squeezer to do it.
2. Now peel the apple with the help of the vegetable peeler. Cut it in half. Do this by putting the apple down on the chopping board, hold it steady with your left hand and cut neatly with your right. Don't try to cut the apple holding it up in the air! Now cut the half in halves again and then chop in small pieces. Put into the bowl with the banana.

86

3. In the same way that you cut the apple, peel and cut the guavas. Remove all the seeds and cut in small pieces. Put it into the bowl with the other fruit.
4. Sprinkle over the salts, *chaat masala* and the red chilli powder if you're using it. Mix it all together well with a big spoon. Now taste it and see if you need to add anything. You might need to add some more lemon juice or a pinch of sugar. If it's not needed, serve the *chaat* out into two bowls and what did you say? you're going to eat it all yourself? Well, good appetite!

Note: When pomegranate (*anaar*) is in season, it makes an excellent addition to this *chaat*.

Fruit Mouse

ALU-PAPRI CHAAT
A Crunchy Potato-curds Combination

Tell your family you're going to make this and I bet they won't believe you! Just prove them wrong!

You Will Need for FOUR People

24 *papris* (you can get these from any good *halwai*)
4 small potatoes,
1 cup curds (*dahi*)
$1/2$ teaspoon salt
a little *Chaat Masala*
8 teaspoons *sev*

For the Tamarind Chutney (which you should cook and cool before you make the *chaat*)

Tamarind (*imli*), the size of 1 medium potato
Jaggery (*gur*) a little bigger in size than the ball of *imli*
$1/2$ teaspoon black salt
$1/2$ teaspoon ground cumin (*zeera*)
1 tablespoon raisins (*kismis*)
$1\,1/4$ cups water

You will Also Need

two small bowls, a spoon, a knife, a chopping board, a small pan with a handle, another spoon, a plastic bowl, a large plastic strainer, four small serving plates

Alu chaat in the making

A dedicated sandwich-maker, if ever there was one !

And a pretty pizza specialist

Baking a cake ! the weighing

The buttering and flouring

Spell success !

Dishing out a delicious dinner

Getting set to cook rice?

Cooking is serious business !

Nimbu Pani is a sq. . . . u.u.u. . . .eeze !

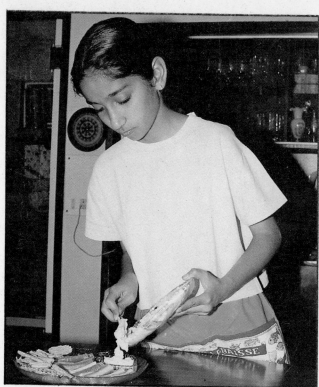

Dip, dip, dip. . .
this one's delicious !

A sandwich house ! Looks too good to eat !

The team of cooks : Before

. . . and after !

Clearing up . . . . the price of fun ?

To Make It

1. Till you make the *chaat,* keep the *papris* in an air-tight box.
2. Boil the potatoes as in the recipe for *Channa-Alu-Chaat.* Cool them then peel and cut into cubes. Put into one of the bowls.
3. In the other bowl, put the curds and mix it smooth with the spoon. You can also do it with an egg-beater if you like. Mix the potatoes into the curds with the salt.
4. Put the *imli* and *gur* into the plastic bowl. Pour $1^1/_4$ cups water over and leave for at least half an hour. After half an hour, put the strainer over the small pan and pour the *imli-gur* mixture into the strainer. The liquid will run through. Now with your hand or a large spoon, press the mixture that's left in the strainer. Keep doing this till only the seeds and some thready part of the *imli* is left behind. This you can throw away. Wash your hands.
5. Put the pan on the fire, on high heat. Hold the pan by the handle and keep stirring till the mixture starts boiling then turn the heat down to low and still stirring, cook the mixture for about 10 minutes by which time it will have become thicker than it was and will be shiny— just the way you know *imli chutny* should look. Add the salt, *zeera* and raisins. Cook for another minute and take off the fire. Leave it to cool then chill it in the refrigerator.
6. Now you're all ready to make your *chaat.* For each person, on a plate, put 6 *papris.* If there are any that are too bumpy, crumble them on the plate. Over the *papris,* pour some of the potato-curds mixture. Over that pour a

89

teaspoon of your delicious *imli chutney*, and sprinkle over a pinch of *chaat masala*. You've seen how the *chaat*-man does it? Take some between your thumb and index finger and go round the plate, sprinkling it! That's it!! You look professional! Finally, sprinkle over the *sev*—about a teaspoon per plate. Serve immediately. Do I need to say that?

Note: If you're too young to cook the chutney yourself, I'm sure some adult will help you do it. Also I must tell you that you certainly won't need so much of it for one time but you can safely keep it in the fridge in a glass bottle and it will not go bad for many weeks. So the next time, you need to make this *chaat*—and I'm sure it's going to be a big success— you can do it almost instantly.

BEST HOME-MADE PIZZA

There couldn't be a simpler way of making pizza. Just remember to buy the bases and before you know it, you'll be sinking your teeth into cheesy, tomatoey pizza, as good as any you can buy in a shop.

You Will Need for ONE Pizza

1 pizza base   1 cube cheese or pizza cheese
Tomato sauce   1 small capsicum

You Will Also Need

an oven tray, a knife and chopping board, a grater, a small bowl, a table-knife, oven gloves, a timer

To Make It

1. Put your oven on. Set it to preheat to 180°C.
2. Wash the capsicum and chop up it into tiny pieces on the chopping board. You can ask an adult for help if you need. Put the cut-up capsicum into a small bowl.
3. Lay one base on the chopping board. Pour some tomato sauce over and spread it evenly all over, right to the edges.
4. Sprinkle little bits of capsicum all over.
5. Grate cheese all over. Hold the grater in your left hand over the pizza and with your right hand, grate the cheese. Pizza chese melts best

but others taste just as good. Use whichever you have at home. If you are using the cubes, use one per base. Put the pizza on the oven-tray. Check that the oven has heated up to 180°C.

6. With your oven glove on, put the tray into the oven. Set your timer for 10 minutes or note the time.

7. Check on your pizza after ten minutes. The top should have browned lightly and the cheese should have melted. If this has not happened, let it be inside for another 5 minutes. Now, in any case, the fragrance will tell you it's done!

Note: At the top, I haven't mentioned how many people this recipe will feed. That's because I don't know how hungry (or greedy) you and your friends are feeling. You know a pizza can be cut into 8 pieces or just 4 or 2 or maybe you feel like having a whole one each. So look at the base, judge your appetite and decide how many you need!

Other Toppings You Can Use

Finely chopped onion, finely chopped ham, salami, cooked left-over mince, cooked chopped sausages, meat or chicken. If you are using the last two, you will have to take the meat off the bone.

ALU TIKKIS
(Potato Cutlets)

Of course you can make *alu tikkis*! At least you're going to do most of the work that's fun—the mashing and squishing and squashing and shaping then just leave the frying to an adult. That's more than a fair deal, isn't it?

You Will Need For TWELVE Tikkis

3 large potatoes,
3 slices bread
a little water
$^3/_4$—1 teaspoon salt

3-4 stalks fresh coriander
$^1/_2$ teaspoon *amchur* (dry mango powder) power
$^3/_4$ teaspoon coriander (*dhaniya*) powder (*dhaniya*)

You Will Also Need

a large plate, preferably one with a narrow edge, a fork, a knife, a chopping board, a shallow bowl, oven gloves

To Make It

1. Boil the potatoes as in the recipe for *Channa Alu Chaat*. Gather all the other things while the potatoes are boiling. You have to get down to work as soon as they're done. You might need to ask an adult for help to chop the fresh coriander finely.
2. Take the hot potatoes out of the cooker after you open it and put them on your counter top.

As soon as you can handle them, using oven gloves, start to peel them. While you're peeling, put the slices of bread in the shallow bowl, covered with water.

3. As soon as you've finished peeling, mash the potatoes roughly in the large plate.

4. One slice at a time, take out the bread from the water and squeeze it hard between the palms of your hands. Squelch! This is fun. When you are sure there's no water left, throw it into the plate with the potatoes. Do the same with the rest of the bread.

5. Now, some more fun. Start mashing. Do it with a fork or your hands. Mash the whole mixture smooth. You should not see any bread separate or any lumps in the potato.

6. Add the salt, corianders, *amchur*—this, by the way, is that deliciously sour dried mango powder. I haven't mentioned chillies but you can add a little red chilli powder or green chillies, finely chopped up, to the mixture.

7. Taste a little bit of the mixture. See if you need to add some more salt.

8. If everything tastes perfect, you can start shaping the *tikkis*. Have fun doing it—make them into flat circles, or sausage shapes or heart shapes for someone special.
Let me tell you how to do it: first, divide your mixture into 12 equal bits. Now take one of the bits in your hand. Roll it into a ball—just like you do your plasticine. Now flatten the ball by pressing it lightly between your palms. Neaten and flatten the edges. Perfect! You have a normal, round *tikki*. Just press with your finger inwards—make a heart shape for me.

Press in at two or thre points along the edge and maybe you would have a pretty flower. Don't make pointed edges though—they might crumble and fall off while they're being fried. When you have made all the *tikkis,* cover the plate with a clean cloth and your part of the deal is done. Now ask an adult to fry them for you.

9. Shall I give you a serving suggestion? Put your round tikki on a plate and with sauce, make two eyes and a big, smiling mouth!

If it's a flower you're serving out, put a big dot of sauce in the centre. And for the heart, how about a border of sauce all around the edge. Do it neatly—put the sauce in a teaspoon (or a plastic bottle with a nozzle (this is a really neat way of doing it) and gently pour it wherever you need. Is your mouth watering? Mine certainly is!

CAN'T-STOP-EATING-IT DIP

Yes, you won't be able to stop eating this until it's all gone. It's easy to make too and you can eat it with lots of things—vegetables, on your toast, with chips.

You Will Need For About 1 Cup

$1^1/_2$ cup of curds (it can be slightly sour)
$^1/_4$ teaspoon salt
$^1/_2$ teaspoon pepper

$1-1^1/_2$ teaspoons sugar, if possible, ground
1-2 tablespoons cheese (if you don't have it at home, try one of the other ideas mentioned below)

You Will Also Need

a large plastic strainer, a bowl, a measuring cup, teaspoons, a large spoon, a plate, a fork.

To Make It

1. Measure out the curds.
2. Put the strainer over the bowl and pour the curds into it. Leave it for about 1 hour.
3. When you come back you will see that the curds in the strainer seems to have shrunk into a creamy ball. The water from the curds will have drained out into the bowl underneath.
4. Put the creamy ball of curds into the plate. Mash it smooth with the fork.
5. Add the salt, pepper, sugar and cheese if you're using it. Mix it all smooth.

96

6. Taste and add whatever is needed—more sugar, perhaps or a little more pepper. If it's just fine, put it into a small, pretty serving bowl and keep it in the fridge till you're ready to eat it.
7. To serve it, put the serving bowl in the centre of a big plate and surround it with chips or vegetables—like carrots, radishes, cauliflower in the winter and cucumber in the summer. Of course you have to peel the vegetables—remember our friend, the vegetable peeler? Use her then wash the vegetables well and cut them into long sticks or circles.

Note: To make this dip different each time you make it, here's what you can do:
Add a teaspoon or two of tomato sauce to it or a little bit of mustard, or some grated ginger or finely chopped capsicum. Try them all.

Vegetables

97

CHEESE STICKS

This must be one of the most fun-filled recipes in the whole book. You've got to make the dough, in itself a squishy, squashy fun-experience, then you have to roll it out, which I know you're always longing to do, then you have to shape it and finally, you even have to paint it. Does this sound like an art and craft project rather than a cookery one? Well, its both. Have fun!

You Will Need For 4-6 People

100 grams (little less than 1/2 cup)
butter, if possible white
7 tablespoons flour $^1/_2$ teaspoon pepper
$^1/_2$ teaspoon salt   a little *zeera* or *ajwain*
2 boiled potatoes   Food colours

You Will Also Need

a plastic strainer or wheat-sifter, a large plate to make the dough, a pressure cooker to boil the potatoes, a fork, cling-film or a plastic box, a chopping board, a rolling pin, oven-trays, biscuit cutters in different shapes, a knife, small bowls, a new or very clean-paint-brush, oven gloves, a timer.

To Make It

1. Take the butter out of the fridge and keep it out to soften.
2. First of all, sift the flour. Put it into the plastic strainer and shake into the large plate. All the

clean flour will go down and you will see the bits of rubbish that were in it 'caught' on top. Throw it away.

3. Mash the potatoes (you know how to boil them already don't you?) Put them into the plate with the flour. Also add the salt and pepper and the butter. If it has not softened completely, put it into a little pan and keep on the fire for a few minutes then add it in. With your hand, start mixing all the things in the plate together. When it is all nicely mixed, wrap a piece of cling film around it or put it into the plastic box. Put it away into the fridge for about half an hour. This will help it to harden a little so you can roll it out easily.

4. Now take it out of the fridge and after putting flour all over your board (you can also do it on a clean counter top) start rolling it out. Roll with the rolling-pin, like you've seen *chappatis* being made till you feel the dough is even all over. Dont make it too thin.

5. Put the oven on preheat to 180°c.

6. Now it's time to cut out some interesting shapes. Press your cookie-cutters down into the dough. Come on, be imaginative—make a bird, a girl, a boy, a star, a flower—just whatever shapes you have. As you cut a shape, gently lift it out (with the help of a knife) and lay it in your oven tray. When you have no more place left on your dough sheet, just gather up all the dough left on the board or counter and roll it out again and start again. You will need more than one oven tray. If you don't have it, just lay the shapes on a plate and you can transfer them after the first batch is baked.

99

7. When you've cut out all the shapes, you can paint them if you like. Yes, paint them. Put some food colour into a little bowl, mix a little water into it, dip your brush in and paint your shapes—green wings for your bird, a colourful *ghagra* for your girl, smart shorts for your boy—you can use all the colours you have at home but remember they must be good food colours and not normal paints. You can buy them in tiny bottles at any grocer's shop. In case you don't want to paint, sprinkle over the *zeera* and *ajwain* over the cheese-shapes and you're ready to bake them.

8. When your oven tells you it's ready and heated, put in the first tray. Bake 10–15 minutes or till the cheese shapes are golden brown in colour. If you've got the timer, set it for 10 minutes then you can peek in and see if you need to keep them in for an extra 5 minutes.

9. When they're done, take them out carefully, wearing your oven gloves of course and let them cool. Put in the next batch. Those of you who are not allowed to handle the oven, please have the rest of the fun and tell an adult to do the last few stages for you.

By the way, are you wondering why these are called Cheese shapes when there is not a shred of cheese in the recipe? Well, that's the magical part. Just you taste them and you'll agree there couldn't be a better name for them!

Note: In case some day, you're not feeling inspired enough to shape and paint, you can just cut the dough into sticks or diamonds. Also, if you want to make it more spicy, you can add some chilly powder to the dough.

BUN-SAMOSA

Now, this strange sounding snack is something I enjoyed thoroughly in my school-days. The crunch and spice of the *samosa*, the soft buttery bun, the saucy taste all go so well. Do try it.

You Will Need For ONE Bun-Samosa

1 burger bun	some butter
1 *samosa*	some tomato sauce

You Will Also Need

a chopping board or plate, a knife

For Make It

1. Holding the bun down on the plate with one hand, cut it in half, leaving a little bit joined at the end.
2. Butter the bun and pour some sauce over both sides. Spread it out.
3. Slightly smash the samosa. Stuff it into the bun. Press it closed. Eat it. Now tell m honestly, don't you feel like making yourself another one?

FAIRYTALE FANTASIES

I bet you can't guess what this chapter's all about. And shall I tell you another thing you probably haven't guessed—that's the amount of fun you're going to have, not only making these wonderful desserts, but also telling the stories behind some of them to your younger friends. I'm sure they're your very favourite desserts too—ice-creams and jellies. There are some other delicious ideas too for ways to end your meal in style. Oh yes, I can see that you're going to enjoy cooking and eating and so are all those you are going to do it for.

Sould we start? Shall I give you the usual little lecture I do telling you the better way to do it?! Well, there's really nothing to making jelly except for one or two things you might like to remember. When you mix the hot water into the jelly crystals, remember to stir it well. Go round and round briskly with your spoon till there are no lumps left and the liquid in your bowl looks really clear. Only then add the cold water and again mix well otherwise you might have lumps in your jelly. Ugh!

Also, remember a jelly made for 4 persons (1 packet) will take at least 5-6 hours to set. So don't be impatient and if you're planning to serve it for lunch, don't start making it after breakfast— do it the evening before.
The only part that is a little tricky about jelly desserts is taking them out of their setting dishes without making a mess. Here's how to do it:

1. After your jelly is well set, take it out of the fridge. Put it down on the counter-top or table.
2. Keeping it steady with one hand, take a round-bladed knife and run it all along the edge of the jelly, to loosen it slightly along the edge.
3. Now put a plate on top of the jelly-bowl, making sure it (the bowl) is in the centre.
4. Put your right hand on the bottom of the plate, which is upwards now. Slide your left hand under the bowl and turn it over. It isn't as complicated as it sounds. You can practice with an empty, preferably unbreakable bowl before you start. Now you have the plate on the counter and the bowl upside down on it.
5. If it's summer, leave the jelly for 5 minutes then slide both your hands under the plate and hold the jelly bowl with your thumbs. Pick up the plate and bowl and shake gently. Soon you should hear a Whump! Put the plate down.
6. Carefully lift the bowl and you should see your jelly sitting pretty on the plate. No? It's still cozy in the bowl. O.K, then try this: Dip a small hand towel in hot water, squeeze it out (careful!) and lay it over the top of the bowl for a minute. Now again, pick up the plate and bowl as you did before and shake! Did you hear the Whump! Good!
7. Now you can go on and decorate your jelly if you like. By the way, this hot-towel sauna for your jelly is what will aways be needed if you're making it in winter. You can ask an adult to handle it if neded.

As far as ice-creams go, we're going to really make them the stuff of dreams. Lets use nuts, and chocolate sauce (of course, you're going to make it), a drizzle of honey, maybe or crushed pepper-mints to add a whole new dimension to your favorite ice-cream. I can't wait to get started. Just remember one thing, though.

Keep all the things you need for your ice-cream fantasy ready before you serve otherwise you might have milk-shake instead of ice-cream!

O.K, I can hear you getting impatient now, so let's not waste any more time. First, the jellies.

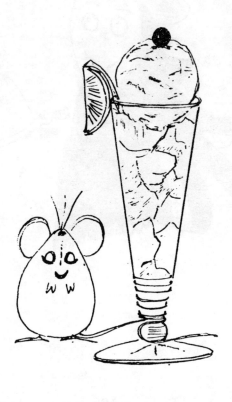

PRETTY MISS JELLY

You have to make this pretty Miss to believe how pretty she looks! You will enjoy doing it, I know.

You Will Need For FOUR People

1 packet jelly, any
flavour
decorations*

1 cup hot water
1 cup cold water
a few teaspoons butter
or *malai*.

You Will Also Need

a cake-pan, about 6" in diameter, a bowl, a tablespoon, and later, a plain serving plate

To Make It

1. Put the jelly crystals into the bowl. Pour the hot water over. Mix well with the tablespoon till the liquid is absolutely clear.
2. Add the cold water. Mix and stir again.
3. Pour into the cake-pan. Put into the fridge and let it set for at least 6 hours.

---

*Gems, nutties, sweets in the shape of a ring, silver balls, coloured *saunf*, small chocolate biscuits or wafers—just whatever you like to use and not necessarily all of these. Plan out your Pretty Miss (draw her out if you like) and then see what you need to get for her.

4. Unmould as I explained in the introduction. Fantastic, you have a beautiful round jelly sitting on your plate.

5. Now, lets make her into a Pretty Miss.

Put two small chocolate biscuits for her eyes or cut out two circles from the wafers. You can do this with a clean scissor.

Now, lets put two gems in the middle—the same coloured ones, of course. Stick them down with a dot of *malai* or butter.

Do the same with another gem for her nose and what about her mouth? Use a peppermint or any ring-shaped sweet. Then her hair—use some nutties or gems, make her a bow if you like cut from the wafers. And don't forget her earrings—two upturned lollipops will do. Push a little bit of the stick into the jelly.

Gosh, she looks too pretty to eat, doesn't she? Wouldn't it be just super to serve her if you're having a little party? Of course, you may need to use more packets of jelly.

Also, remember, you can't do the decorations too much in advance as the colours may start running and Pretty Miss doesn't like looking messy!

*The decorations could include gems.

STRIPED JELLY

This recipe is only for those kids who have patience and are prepared to spend some hours watching the jelly at different stages. This was Goldilocks favourite too, you know and what her mother was working at when Goldilocks just slipped out and went off to have her own adventure. Try it, in the holidays, perhaps— it does look so pretty.

You Will Need For SIX People

2 packets jelly, in different colours
1 cup hot water

3 cups cold water
$^1/_2$ cup cream, if you like

You Will Also Need

a jelly mould which takes at least 4 cups liquid, 2 bowls, 2 spoons, 2 napkins or 2 small plates

To Make It

1. Open one packet of jelly. Pour it into one of the bowls and pour the hot water over. Stir well till the liquid is absolutely clear.
2. Add one cup of the cold water. Stir again and pour in about one third of the liquid into the jelly mould. Leave the rest of it out on the countertop covered with a napkin or plate. Put the mould into the fridge. Leave it there for 1 hour.

3. Peek after the hour is over. If the jelly has begun to set, open the second packet and make the jelly as you did earlier, first adding 1 cup hot water then 1 cup cold. Pour about one-third of this liquid over the first in the mould. The first jelly should be set enough so the colours don't mix. Put it back into the fridge for an hour. Take out and add the alternate colour—get the idea? Make as many stripes as you have the patience for! If this sounds like too much trouble, just make 4 stripes—that means first put half of the first jelly, then half of the second, then the remaining lot of the first and finally, the remaining lot of the second. It looks lovely enough too.

4. When all the stripes of jelly have set, you can unmould it. You remember I told you how to do it in the introduction? It is best to make this jelly a day before you want to serve it.

5. If you're using the cream, pour it over before serving or serve it separately so everyone can admire the stripes better before they eat.

PRETTY, PINK JELLY

"Of course, you will go to the ball," said Cinderella's fairy godmother as she appeared suddenly in her kitchen, "and certainly, you shall have a special dress in your favourite colour pink. And not only will you have a special dress, you shall even see at the ball a jelly to match your clothes—pale pink with silver balls on it....."
Will you make it? Of course, you will!

You Will Need For FOUR People

1 packet raspberry or strawberry jelly
$^{1}/_{2}$ cup hot water
Silver balls*

1 cup cold water
$^{1}/_{2}$ cup cream or top-of-the-milk (malai)

You Will Also Need

a jelly mould, a bowl, a hand or electric beater and if you're using malai, a bowl and fork

To Make It

1. Put the jelly crystals into the bowl. Pour over the hot water. Stir well till the liquid is absolutely clear.
2. Add the cold water. Again, stir well. Pour into the jelly mould. Put into the fridge for at least $1^{1}/_{2}$ hours.
3. After $1^{1}/_{2}$ hours, peek in and see if the jelly is

111

beginning to set. Take it out and with the beater, beat it almost smooth, adding the cream as you beat. If you're using *malai,* make it smooth first by putting it into the small bowl and mixing it with the fork. When the jelly looks a pretty pink, pour it back into the mould and put back into the fridge 3 to allow it to set fully.

4. When the jelly is set, unmould as I explained in the introduction. Decorate with silver balls.

Note: If you don't have the silver balls at home, leave them out though they do look so pretty if you can get them.

VERY SPECIAL ICE-CREAM JELLY

Yes, this is exactly what it's all about—two favourites in one. Hard to believe? Can't wait to try it out? Well, that is what I expected you to say!

You Will Need For FOUR (not very hungry) People

1 packet orange jelly $^1/_2$ cup hot water
2 cups vanilla ice-cream

You Will Also Need

a small bowl to dissolve the jelly crystals, a serving bowl a spoon, an electric or hand-beater.

To Make It

1. Empty the jelly crystals into the small bowl.
2. Pour the hot water over the crystals and stir with the spoon till the liquid is absolutely clear. Cover and leave to cool then put into the fridge for $1^1/_2$ hours.
3. Peek at the jelly after $1^1/_2$ hours. It should be beginning to set. With the electric or hand beater, gently beat it up, adding the ice-cream as you do so. When it is smoothly mixed, pour into the serving bowl and put it back into the fridge to chill well.

Of course you can try other flavours of jelly and ice-cream for example, lemon jelly with vanilla or pista ice-cream, strawberry with chocolate, raspberry with butterscotch or—I'm sure you're better than me at this wonderful combining of flavours!

BANANA-LEMON JELLY

Oh, yes, you bet this has a story about it too! This, is the jelly that wicked witch gave Hansel to eat, to fatten him up. Remember when she had him locked up and was giving him all kinds of delicious things to eat? Well, lemon-banana jelly was one of them topped with a generous dollop of cream of course. Well, Hansel may not have felt like eating it but I'm sure you'll enjoy it thoroughly!

You Will Need For FOUR People

1 packet lemon jelly

1 cup hot water
1 cup cold water
2 bananas

$^1/_2$ cup cream or top-of-the-milk(*malai*)
$^1/_2$ lemon

You Will Also Need

a bowl, a jelly mould, a knife, a chopping board, a lemon squeezer, a small bowl and fork if you're using *malai*, and later, a pretty serving plate

To Make It

1. Put the jelly crystals into the bowl. Pour over the hot water. Mix well till the liquid is absolutely clear.
2. Pour in the cold water. Again, stir well.
3. Peel the bananas. Lay one at a time on the

115

chopping board and cut into slices that are neither too thick nor too thin. Sprinkle the slices with lemon juice. Use the squeezer to take it out. Put the slices prettily all along the bottom of the jelly mould.

4. Now pour the jelly liquid over the bananas. Don't get upset if some of them get frisky and start swimming around. You can push them down a little later when the jelly begins to set somewhat, after about 2 hours. Leave the jelly in the top shelf of the fridge to set fully, which will take at least 6 hours.

5. When it is fully done, you can unmould it as I told you in the introduction. Pour the cream over just before serving. If you're using *malai*, put it into the small bowl and beat it smooth with a fork. If you have people who you know don't like to eat cream, serve it separately.

RED RIDING HOOD SPECIAL

You remember how Red Riding Hood's mother told her to go off straight to her grandmother's house and not lose herself on the way? Well, one of the reasons she told her to hurry along was because in her basket, wrapped up well was this jelly. "Go and put it straight into the fridge," she told her, and then, when you turn it out for lunch, both Grandmother and you will have a laugh because, the jelly too has a red hood—just like you!"

You Will Need for FOUR people (no wolves invited!)

I packet raspberry or strawberry jelly
1 cup hot water

1 cup cold water
2 tablespoons cream or top-of-the-milk (*malai*)

You Will Also Need

a jelly mould, a tablespoon, a hand or electric beater, one bowl, and later, a pretty serving plate.

To Make It

1. Put the jelly crystals into the bowl. Pour over the hot water. With the tablespoon, mix well so you can see a clear liquid.
2. Put in the cold water. Mix well again. Pour half the liquid into the jelly mould. Let the rest of the liquid remain in the mixing bowl. Put

117

both mould and bowl into the fridge. Leave for
$1^1/_2$ hours.

3. After $1^1/_2$ hours, peek and see that the jellies
have just begun to set. If they have, take out
the one in the mixing bowl, beat it up with the
hand or electric beater, add the cream as you
beat (if you are using *malai,* make it smooth
first) and then pour this mixture over the half-
set plain jelly in the mould. Put back in the
fridge to set fully.

Yes, you've guessed it! When you turn the jelly
out, you'll have a pink jelly topped with a red
hood—just like the heroine of this recipe!

Now won't you have fun telling this to the little
kids you make this for.

BREAD PUDDING

"Oh, I do feel hungry," exclaimed the Sleeping Beauty as she woke up after hundred years (can **you** imagine sleeping that long?), "I'd love some piping hot Bread Pudding. With raisins or maybe jam or ..... "Then she noticed the Prince standing there, looking at her and she almost forgot how hungry she was!
You won't do that, will you? Just rush along and make this absolutely delicious dessert.

You Will Need For FOUR People

4 slices bread	1 handful raisins or some jam
some white butter, slightly softened by taking it out of the fridge half-an-hour before you make the dessert	2 eggs
	$1^3/_4$ tablespoons sugar
	$1^3/_4$ cups milk
	$^1/_2$ teaspoon vanilla essence

You Will Also Need

a knife, a chopping board, a small bowl (it could be a plastic one), a small pan with a handle, medium sized oven-proof serving bowl with a flat bottom, a fork, a strainer, a timer.

To Make It

1. Cut the crusts off the slices of bread. Of course, you know how to do it. You learnt it in the section on sandwiches, didn't you?

119

2. Butter the bread. If you are not using the raisins, also spread jam over each slice. Cut each slice into 4 squares. Lay the squares in the serving bowl. If you're using the raisins, sprinkle them over.

3. Put the milk in the pan and put the pan on the fire. Stir it gently. As soon as you see bubbles along the sides, you can take the milk off.

4. While the milk is heating, put the eggs and sugar into the small bowl. (You do remember how to break an egg? If you don't, turn to the first few pages of the book). Mix well with a fork. Pour the milk over and stir well so that the sugar melts. Add the vanilla essence.

5. Through the strainer, pour this egg-milk mixture over the bread in the bowl. Leave it to sit for at least 15 minutes, and turn the oven on to preheat to 180°c.

6. When the oven is heated up, put your dessert in, set your timer for 45 minutes and wait patiently.

7. Remember it will be very hot, so ask an adult for help to take it out of the oven. Serve immediately with cream (if you're feeling greedy or as hungry as the Sleeping Beauty!)

FUN-TOPPINGS FOR ICE-CREAMS

Here, children, are some fun-things you can do to pretty up your ice-creams. Just buy your favourite flavour of ice-cream and stop! don't tear off the cover and gobble it up—let's make it really a dream come true. Here are some ideas. First, of course, you've guessed right—let's make some chocolate sauce.

You Will Need For FOUR Greedy Children Who Want To Eat More Sauce Than Ice-Cream

$^3/_4$ cup ground sugar
$^1/_3$ cup water
3 tablespoons cocoa

1 teaspoon coffee
2 teaspoons cornflour
2-3 teaspoons water

You Will Also Need.

a small pan with a handle, a wooden or metal spoon, a small bowl or *katori*, a teaspoon, cling-film

To Make It

1. Put the sugar, water, cocoa and coffee into the pan with the handle. Set it on the fire over a medium flame. Stir it as it heats up with the wooden or other spoon. It should become a smooth sauce. Cook it for 7 minutes.
2. While the sauce is cooking, stop stirring it for a second to do this: put the cornflour into the small bowl or *katori*, put the few teaspoons of water into it and stir it into a smooth paste. Go back to stirring the sauce on the fire.

121

3. When the sauce has cooked for **7** minutes, take it off the fire for a second, stir the cornflour into it and set it back on the fire. Keep stirring for a few more minutes till the sauce looks thick and shiny—just like chocolate sauce should. If you're serving hot chocolate sauce, pour it into a pretty jug or bowl and put it on the table immediately. If you have some left over, keep it away in the fridge after it's cooled for another session of ice-cream eating. Cover it with cling-film or even a plate and it can keep in the fridge for weeks. However, when you take it out the next time, remember it might look thicker than you might want it so you can add a few teaspoons of water to it when you're heating it.

MORE ICE-CREAM MAKE-UP

How about topping your favourite ice-cream with some of these ideas?

1. Finely chopped up nuts—you can use walnuts, almonds or even cashews.
2. Grated chocolate or just chocolate broken up into bits. (You know how to grate it, of course? With the same grater you use for cheese and so many other things)
3. Crushed up biscuit crumbs, specially chocolate or ginger biscuits
4. Left-over cake, crumbled
5. Crushed pepper mints. This is simply fantastic over chocolate ice-cream
6. A teaspoon of honey and some nuts
7. A teaspoon of drinking chocolate, or any milk flavouring
8. A teaspoon of coffee. This is my favourite
9. A teaspoon of any squash
10. A mixture of any of these.

To Make It

1. Of course, you know already how to go about this. Put your scoop of ice-cream in a small bowl or plate, and sprinkle over any of the toppings.
2. To make a **Special Sundae,** add the nuts, a teaspoon of squash and some chocolate sauce.
3. To make a **Banana Split,** in a quarter plate, lay a banana split in half (lengthwise, of course,)

and on each half, put half a cup each of two
different ice-creams, put the rest of the ice-
cream on the other half, and top both with
nuts, honey if you like and chocolate sauce of
course. This sounds like a meal by itself.

Did I hear one of you say "of course not?"

Banana Split

Honey Toppling with Nuts

124

APPLE CRUMBLE

"What lovely apples, "sighed Snow White as she looked out of the window and saw the old lady with a basket full of the most perfect looking ones. "They're just perfect to make the Apple Crumble that Grumpy and Dopey and Sneezy all love. I think I'll get some. . . .

"Well, we all know what happened to *her* but I'm sure you'll love eating double helpings of this and all that'll happen to you is that you'll feel very full and satisfied!

You Will Need For FOUR People

5 big apples
1 lemon
a small piece of
cinnamon (*dalchini*)

$^1/_2$ cup sugar, if possible ground
$3^1/_2$ tablespoons flour
some cream, if you like
$^1/_4$ cup butter

You Will Also Need

a potato peeler, a chopping board, a sharp fruit knife, a lemon squeezer, an oven—proof serving dish with a flat bottom, an *atta* strainer, a large plate, if possible one that has shallow sides, oven gloves, a timer.

To Make It

1. If you are going to eat the dessert soon after you make it, put the oven on to preheat to 180°c.
2. Peel the apples and cut them into little bits. To peel them, you can use the potato peeler and

go round the whole apple. Then, put it down on the chopping board, stem side up, hold it with your left hand and cut through the centre with the knife. Cut the halves again into halves and the slices into bits. Keep dropping them into the oven-proof bowl you have chosen.

After you have cut about two apples, squeeze some lemon juice over (with the help of the squeezer, of course) so that they don't go brown. Then continue cutting and squeeze the rest of the juice over when you have finished all the cutting. Stir the apples around so they all get licked by the juice.

Put the piece of cinnamon down amongst the apple bits.

3. Now, for some fun. Put the sugar into the large plate. Over it, sift (that means strain) the flour over through the *atta*-strainer. (If you've forgotten how to do it, take a peek at the first few pages of the book.)

   Put the butter also into the plate. It is more fun if it is not too soft. Now, start rubbing with your fingers—rub the butter into the flour and sugar. As you go along, it will start looking like fat crumbs. When the whole plateful looks life that, you can stop. The fun's over! Sprinkle the crumbs evenly over the apples in the dish.

4. By now, your oven should be heated up.
   With oven gloves on, put the dish into the oven. Shut the door.

5. Put your timer on to 45 minutes and while your dessert is baking, clear up the mess you've made in the kitchen.

   After 45 minutes, your Crumble should look golden brown and smell heavenly of gooey

apples and cinnamon. With your oven gloves
on, take it out and serve it with the cream, if
you're deciding to use it.

6. By the way, if you're being very organised and
making the dessert in the morning but are
going to eat it only in the evening, what you
could do is make the flour and butter mixture
earlier, store it in the fridge and then just before
baking, chop up the apples and sprinkle it
over. It fact, you can even make double the
quantity mentioned here and keep half of it
away in a bottle in the fridge to use another
time.

IRRESISTIBLE CHOCOLATE DREAM

Smooth, creamy, as bitter as you like to make it, this chocolate desert is quite dreamy. Its easy and quick to make too. I have a feeling it must have been invented in Willie Wonkas Chocolate Factory. You try it and decide!

You Will Need For FOUR Small Servings

$2^1/_2$ cups milk
$3^1/_2$ tablespoons sugar
$2^1/_2$ tablespoons cocoa
$^1/_2$ tablespoon cornflour

a few drops vanilla essence
decorations if you want them
—silver balls or multi-coloured *saunf*

You Will Also Need

a small pan with a handle, a small bowl, a teaspoon, a serving bowl, a wooden spoon or a tablespoon to cook the pudding, a metal net cover or napkin

To Make It

1. Put the milk and sugar into the handled pan and put it on the fire. Stir as the milk starts heating up to dissolve the sugar.
2. While the milk is heating up, do this: put the cocoa and cornflour into the small bowl and with a few teaspoons of milk, (you can even take it from the pan) stir the cocoa and flour into a smooth paste. Do this with the help of a teaspoon.

128

3. As soon as the paste is smooth, and the milk is heated (you will be able to see bubbles around the edges), pour the cocoa into the milk on the fire. With the wooden spoon or tablespoon, stir continuously till the mixture thickens and you can see it coating the spoon. Take it off the fire and stir in the essence.

4. Pour it into the serving dish and leave it out on the counter-top, covered with a metal net cover or napkin. When it has cooled, you can put it into the fridge to chill well.

5. Serve decorated with the balls or *saunf*.

Note: If you like the dessert to be thinner and more like a custard add $^1/_2$ cup more milk.
If you want it more bitter, add $^1/_2$ teaspoon coffee.
If you want an exotic almond flavour, add a few drops almond essence.

LIGHT-AS-AIR MANGO DESSERT

You will just love making this dessert—for yourself and others in your family. Your kid sister or brother, your grandmother—all will love it equally. It is so light, so melt-in-the-mouth and just so simple to make. The most difficult part of the recipe, perhaps, is asking for permission to use the blender!

You Will Need For FOUR People

3 large mangoes
4-5 tablespoons milk
4 tablespoons cream or
top-of-the-milk (malai)

4 cubes ice
Sugar

You Will Also Need

a knife, a spoon, a chopping board, a clean napkin, a serving bowl or individual serving cups, a blender

To Make It

1. Wash the mangoes well and put one on the chopping board. Cut it into slices. Do you know how to do that? Hold the mango down on the board with your left hand and cut with your right. You should be cutting on both sides of the seed. Slice all the mangoes then scoop the flesh out of them. You can do it easily with a spoon. As you scoop, drop the flesh straight into the blender.

2. Into the blender also put the cream and milk. Add 4 tablespoons first. Also add the sugar. Start with adding 4 teaspoons.

3. Wrap the ice-cubes in the clean napkin and hit it (not too hard!) on the counter-top. Soon you will have crushed ice. Drop it into the blender too. Whizz the blender for half a minute. You will be able to see all the things inside mixing up well. Open the blender and take a little mixture out in a spoon and taste it. See if it needs more sugar or if it is too thick, add some more milk. Stir it and whizz for just a few seconds more. Check if everything seems perfect now.
I'm sure it does so stop making excuses to taste it again!

4. Pour it into the serving bowl or cups and put it into the fridge till you're ready to eat.

*By the way, if you don't have cream or *malai* at home, make the recipe without it. Instead, add a little more milk so you have a nice, creamy mixture.

PEACHES N' ICE-CREAM

Another super simple dessert that's really delicious. Its one of those lazy ones too that you have to just put together!

You Will Need For Each Serving

2 peach halves   1 cup vanilla ice-cream
I walnut or some silver balls

You Will Also Need

pretty serving plates, a tin-opener, a nut-cracker if you're using unshelled walnuts,

To Make It

1. Open the tin of peach-halves. You would do well to buy a large tin if you're planning to make the dessert for at least 4 people.
2. Onto each plate put two peach halves.
3. Into each half, put half the ice-cream from the cup, smoothing it neatly on the top. Pour over a teaspoon of syrup from the tin.
4. Put a walnut half on top of the ice-cream or sprinkle over some silver balls, if you're using them instead.
5. Serve your dessert immediately. This is really a last-minute dessert so make sure you have everything handy before you start.

Note: By the way, though vanilla ice-cream goes really well with peaches, of course, you can try other flavours of ice-cream too. Also, depending on the size of the peach-halves in the tin, you might have some left over. Keep them away (not in the tin) in the fridge to enjoy the next day.

VERY SPECIAL BANANA CREAM

Yes, this banana cream is special, yet so simple. Just a little touch, almost like a waving of a magic wand makes it out-of-the-ordinary.

You Will Need For FOUR People

10 ginger or creamless chocolate biscuits*
1 cup cream or top-of-the milk (*malai*)

4 bananas
4-5 teaspoons sugar

You Will Also Need

a pretty serving dish, a chopping board or plate, a knife, a rolling pin, a bowl, a fork

To Make It

1. Crush the biscuits. Do this by laying them on the plate or chopping board (lay out as many as will fit easily) and gently bash them with the rolling pin. They should start looking like fat crumbs. Another way of doing this is to put them into a clean plastic bag and bash gently with the rolling pin.
2. Put about three-quarters of the crumbs at the bottom of the serving dish. It would be better if it is a flat-bottomed one.
3. Put the cream into the bowl. If you are using *malai*, you will have to beat it smooth, with a

fork. You might also need to add a little milk if it is too dry. Add the sugar to it and beat till it is thick and fluffy. You could use an egg-beater to do this.

4. Peel the bananas and chop them up into slices. As you finish one, drop it into the cream. Do the same with the other three.

5. Mix the bananas with the cream and gently pour them over the biscuit crumbs in the dish.

6. Just before serving, sprinkle the rest of the crumbs over the top, so they are still crunchy when you serve your dessert.

Note: You can also use left-over chocolate cake, crumbled up or Fantastic Fudge Squares instead of the biscuits. Isn't that a good idea?

TRULY SCRUMPTIOUS DELIGHTS

Here, next, is a chapter full of my favourite things—all of them truly scrumptious. You just have to try the Jam Nests—they're such fun to make and of course, I don't expect you to leave out the irresistible Chocolate Chews. Then, you'll come upon Fantastic Fudge Squares—and certainly, by the time you finish with this chapter, I hope you'll have perfected that cake too. It's named after you and truly one of the simplest and most delicious ones I have ever tasted. Don't tell me you've never baked anything, and you just can't imagine baking a cake! Just go ahead, read the recipe—now you can see there's nothing complicated about it at all. Bake it and you might soon hear remarks something like this:

"Wow, since when did *you* become such a good cook?" or

"Hey, I must say this is good! (between mouthfuls, of course). Did you really make this yourself?" Or how about something like this, which would make *me* really happy:

"Pass up that book. If it's got recipes for such things in it, maybe I better get myself a copy."

Have fun, then, making all these little extra treats, the special touches that everyone is sure to appreciate, and devour. (By the way, that means eat up hungrily and greedily as if, yes, as if the food *were* going to run away!)

LITTLE JAM NESTS

These are such fun to make—and perhaps, even more fun to eat. They're rolled, baked and then filled with a dot of your favourite jam. Mixed fruit, is it?!

You Will Need To make about

1 1/2 cups flour
little less than 1/2 teaspoon salt
3/4 cup soft butter
1/4 cup plus 1 tablespoon ground sugar

2 eggs (you will be using only the yolks)*
1 teaspoon vanilla essence
Jam

You Will Also Need

an *atta* strainer, a plastic or other bowl to mix the dough, a small plate and bowl to separate the egg, an electric beater, a biscuit tray, oven gloves, timer, a wooden or metal spoon

To Make It

1. Sift the flour with the salt. If you have forgotten how to do it, the first few pages of the book will remind you. Also separate the egg. The same pages will help.
2. Put the oven on to preheat to 180°C.
3. Put the butter and sugar into the mixing bowl. Beat well with the electric beater till the mixture is smooth. Drop in the egg yolks, one at a

139

time. Beat after each one. Mix in the vanilla and then the flour. You can do this with a wooden or metal spoon. Beat for just a few seconds to make the mixture really smooth.

4. Take a dab of butter on two fingers and rub all over the biscuit tray.

5. Divide the mixture into about 24 bits. Squeeze each bit together. The dough looks crumbly but it will stick together.

6. Now for the fun. Roll each little bit of dough into a ball. Make it nice and smooth and round. Flatten slightly so it looks like a fat *tikki*. Hold it in your left hand and gently, press into its middle with your index finger. You've made a nest. Lay it down in the biscuit tray. Keep rolling, placing the nests about on inch away from each other. (You might have to bake in batches since I am sure all your nests will not fit on one tray.) When the oven is heated, put on your oven gloves and put the first tray in. Smaller kids can ask for help, to do this.

7. Set the timer to 20 minutes. When it rings, your nests should look golden brown. If they do not, leave in the oven for another 5 minutes then take out (with your gloves on). Leave them to cool and then take out one by one and put onto a plate.

8. Just before serving, fill the centers with jam.

*With the whites that are left over, you could make Peppermints.

SATISFYING RAISIN BUNS

Yes, you can make these too and not only have them for tea but you could also take them in your tiffin or gulp one before you rush off to school. Have them as they are or slice them and butter them and—— Mmmmm, my mouth is beginning to water!

You Will Need for about ONE DOZEN buns

1 cup minus 1 tablespoon flour
$3/4$ teaspoon baking powder
6 tablespoons butter

$1/2$ teaspoon vanilla essence
6 tablespoons ground sugar
2 eggs
3-4 teaspoons raisins

You Will Also Need

an atta strainer, a plate, a large plastic or glass bowl, a baking tray, oven gloves, a timer, a clean knitting needle, a tablespoon, an electric beater

To Make It

1. Put the oven on to preheat to 200°C.
2. Sift the flour with the baking powder. If you have forgotten how to do it, look in the first few pages of the book.
3. In the bowl, put the butter, essence and sugar. Beat with the electric beater till smooth.
4. Add one egg. Beat some more. Add the second. Beat again.
5. Drop in the raisins with 1 tablespoon of flour.

141

Fold in the rest of the flour with the tablespoon. Folding in means you have to mix in very *gently*, bringing the mixture from the bottom of the bowl up again and again till the flour is well mixed in.

6. Take a dab of butter on two fingers and rub all over the baking tray. With the same tablespoon you used for folding in the flour, drop the mixture on to the tray. Leave a little gap between each mound.

7. Wearing your oven gloves, check that the oven has heated up then put the tray carefully in. Set your timer for 20 minutes.

8. When you look in after 20 minutes, the buns should be golden brown, they should have risen and if you poke them with the knitting needle, the needle should come out dry and not with gooey batter, around it. If it does, keep in the oven another 5-10 minutes.

You can eat the buns warm or cool.

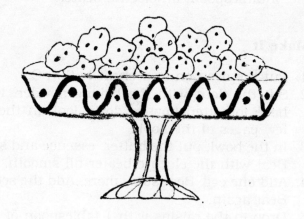

142

CRUNCHY CHOCOLATE CHEWS

You don't like corn-flakes, is it? Well, have you ever tried them coated with chocolate? It's about time you did and maybe, you'll change your mind.

You Will Need for About 20 Balls

2 tablespoons honey
3 small bars or 2 large bars chocolate*

cornflakes
$1^1/_2$ tablespoons butter, if possible unsalted

You Will Also Need

a medium sized pan with a handle, a wooden or metal spoon, a biscuit tray

To Make It

1. Put the honey, butter and chocolate into the pan. Put it on the fire over low heat. Stir every once in a while. As soon as the chocolate is all melted, take it off the fire. Stir it well.
2. Add cornflakes in tablespoonfuls, mixing it as you go .along. Add just as much (about 5-6 tablespoons) so the mixture is neither runny nor too dry.
3. Take a dab of butter on two fingers and rub it all over the bottom of the tray. Take teaspoons of the mixture and drop it onto the tray. Mound.

143

it into a neat ball with your spoon. When all
the mixture is used up, put the tray into the
fridge and leave it there for a couple of hours
or till the mixture is 'set.'

4. Serve on a pretty plate. Are you going to change
your mind about not liking corn-flakes?!

*You can use any chocolate or even a combination
of two different kinds.

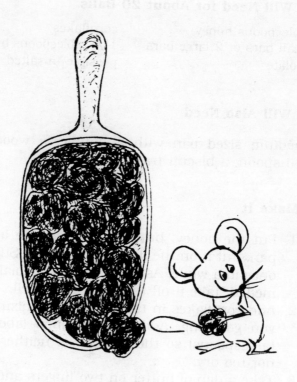

FANTASTIC FUDGE SQUARES

You just have to try these—they are fantastic! And so easy to make too.

You Will Need

8 tablespoons white, unsalted butter
3 tablespoons honey
4 tablespoons cocoa

1 tablespoon sugar
200 grams (1 larger sized packet) of any creamless biscuits*

You Will Also Need

a small pan with a handle, another plastic or glass bowl, a 6-inch square cake-pan or biscuit tray with shallow sides, a wooden spoon or tablespoon, a knife, a mixi or clean plastic bag with a rolling pin.

To Make It

1. Put the butter, honey, cocoa and sugar into the small handled pan. Put it on the fire on low heat. Stir gently with the spoon till the butter melts then stir a little harder to help the sugar to dissolve. Take the pan off the fire.
2. Crush the biscuits. You can put them into the mixi and whizz for a minute or so or you can put them in the plastic bag and gently beat with a rolling pin. Doesn't this sound like fun? Well, do it till the biscuits look like fine crumbs. Put them into the plastic bowl.

3. Pour the butter-cocoa mixture over the biscuit crumbs. Keep mixing with the wooden or metal spoon as you add. If the mixture begins to look too dry you can add some more hony. Mix together well.
4. Pour the mixture you have made into the tray. Press it down with your hands to make it even. Put it into the fridge for about one hour or till the squares set.
5. Take out the tray from the fridge. With the knife, mark it gently into squares. You should get 16-20. Gently take them out of the tray and lay them on a plate. Use a knife if you need to ease them out.

*Note** You can use any biscuits—glucose, ginger or in fact, any sweet, plain ones. Avoid those that have nuts. It is a particularly good idea to make these squares when you have some left-over biscuits that may have gone limp. Even left-over cake crumbs can be used instead of the biscuits.

SPECIAL CAKE

Do you see that space there before special? Well, it's for you to write your name in. Now this cake is named after you and I'm sure all the people in your household are going to beg you to bake it again and again. How about making it too as a surprise when there's a special birthday coming up?

You Will Need For SIX Servings

1 cup minus 1 tablespoon flour
1 teaspoon baking powder
$^1/_2$ cup ground sugar
$^1/_2$ cup butter, preferably white

2 eggs
$^1/_2$ teaspoon vanilla essence
$1^1/_2$ tablespoons cocoa, only if you want a chocolate cake

You Will Also Need

a cake pan—approximately a 6-inch one should do well, an *atta* strainer a wooden or metal spoon, an electric beater, oven gloves, a timer, a knitting needle, a plate, a largeish plastic bowl

To Make It

1. Put the oven on to preheat to 180°C.
2. Sift the flour with the baking powder. If you have forgotten how to do it, take a peek at the first few pages of the book. Put it into the plastic bowl.

147

3. Add all the other things—the butter, sugar, eggs, essence. Add the cocoa if you want a chocolate cake.

4. With the wooden or metal spoon, mix all the things together then beat with the electric beater till you have a smooth batter.

5. Take a dab of butter on two fingers and rub all over the bottom of the cake pan. Over it, drop a teaspoon of flour. Shake the pan so the flour gets stuck evenly all over the buttered bottom. If there is any extra, tap it out by turning the pan over and giving it two sharp hits on the back.

6. Pour the batter into the cake-pan.

7. When the oven is heated up, wearing your oven gloves, put the cake into the oven. (Ask for help if you need.) Set the timer for 35 minutes. Do not peek into the oven before that. When the timer rings, the cake should be risen, browned on top and if you poke a knitting needle into it, it should come out dry, not gooey. If this is not so, leave in for another 10 minutes, then test again. Take the cake out and leave it to cool for 15 minutes. Loosen the cake by running a knife all along the edge.

8. To take out the cake from the pan, wear your oven gloves again, put a plate on top of the pan and smartly, turn it over. Shake it gently and you will feel the cake sliding out. Gently lift away the pan, turn the cake right side up and leave it to cool fully.

Note: This is a small sized cake which should however, make at least 6 good servings. If you want a bigger one, double all the quantities. Remember it will take much longer to bake. Also, for a change, you can add raisins to the cake mixture or the juice of half a lemon if you're making plain cake. When oranges are in season, you can try adding juice from half an orange for a pleasant difference.

To store the cake (if there's any left, which 1 doubt!), put it into an air-tight tin.

BEST HOME-MADE MINTS

Here's idea to use up those egg-whites that you have left over from the jam nests you made. What? You can't imagine making peppermints at home? Well, just try these, and you'll begin to feel a lttle boastful, I'm sure.

You Will Need

1 egg-white*
14 tablespoons icing sugar

a few drops peppermint essence
a few drops red or green food colour, if you like

You Will Also Need

a fork or electric beater, a plastic or glass bowl, a teaspoon, a knife, a tray or plate, and later, an air-tight box.

To Make It

1. Put the egg-white into the bowl. Either with the fork, or electric beater, whip it up till it looks light and frothy,
2. Take out about two tablespoons of the icing sugar and keep it aside. Of the rest, add 8 tablespoons, beating all the time. Also add the essence and food-colour if you're using it. Be very careful though—all you want is pale green or pale pink peppermints not bright green or violent pink. So add just a drop first, beat it in and then see if you need more. Do the same

with the essence. You can decide whether you want very strong or mild mints.

3. On the clean counter-top, drop the two tablespoons sugar you kept aside. Rub it on the surface with your hand. Put the egg-sugar mix on it and knead in the rest of the sugar (4 tablespoons). You know how to knead? Press down on the dough with your knuckles. It will flatten out. Roll it up and repeat. Divide the dough into half. Roll each half into a long roll. Flatten the edges.

4. Lay each roll on the countertop and with a knife, cut into slices. Neaten each mint with a knife or your hand, making the edges smooth. Lay out on a tray or plate. Don't let the mints touch each other. Put into the fridge for at least 5-6 hours or till they're set firm. Now you can put them into an airtight box and after tasting a few, and offering them around, put them back in the fridge to store.

---

*If you have forgotten how to separate an egg, look back to the first ew pages of the book.

MINI-MEALS

I must say, you're getting better and better and I hope, more and more confident. You're well on the way to making meals for yourself and I'm sure, others in your family. Just turn the page and see what interesting meals they are too— Rolls with *Seekh Kababs* in them, Burgers, Spaghetti, even a nice *Pullao*.

Now all you have to do is make one of the things in this chapter and team it with something from the next, which has a selection of Salads and *Raitas*. For example, when you make the *Seekh Kabab* Surprises, team them with one of the salads. The crunchy cucumber one which has peanuts in it goes particularly well. Or, when, you make one of the burgers, perhaps you could serve the Macaroni salad or if you're vegetarian, the one which is made with sprouts. And how does the Saucy Spaghetti sound served with Potato-Pineapple Salad? An interesting meal? I think so.

As for the chickens—the Saucy and Chipsy ones—again, you pick one of the salads, get some nice buns or rolls to go with it and invite a special friend over. You're going to have a super meal. There's another chicken too here, cooked in curds. Now, you could offer to make that when *Makhani Dal* (the black one) is being cooked and perhaps you could even make a *raita* or salad to go with it. You would enjoy doing it and I'm sure the person cooking the meal in your house would appreciate your help.

Talking about *raitas*, they'll go so well with that *pullao*, whenever you decide to make it. Choose a different one each time and see what you enjoy the most.

To make your meal even more complete, you could also make yourself one of those milk-shakes which were one of your first experiments in cooking. And the desserts? Maybe you'd like to make one of them too? To end your meal in style? Yes?

Well, really, I am proud of you!

SEEKH-KABAB SURPRISE

Tired of the usual *dal-roti*? Feel like making a meal of something different? How about trying these? Team with a filling salad from the next section and perhaps a milk-shake and you should soon be feeling happy and full.

You Will Need For FOUR Surprises

4 cooked or half-cooked
*Seekh kababs**
$1^1/_2$ tablespoons oil
2 tablespoons tomato sauce
1 small onion

some white vinegar
4 long dinner rolls
butter
4 tooth-picks

You Will Also Need

a knife, a chopping board, a small *karhai*, a small bowl.

To Make Them

1. If you are using half-cooked *kababs*, first cut them up, approximately the same size as the rolls you've bought. Now cook them. Put the *karhai* on the fire. Put in the oil. Let it heat for 5 minutes.

---

*You can get the half-cooked ones at food-stores or at some butchers'. Since they are sold in different sizes, you might not need 4.

155

2. Drop in the sauce. Stir hard for 2 minutes. You will see the oil is separating out to the sides as the sauce settles in the centre.

3. Put in the *kababs*. Cover the *karhai* with a lid and leave it on a slow fire for 10 minutes. The *kababs* will cook in their own liquid which will soon evaporate. When you peek into the *karhai* after 10 minutes, you should see the *kababs* sitting in the oil. Toss them about lightly so they get fried. Take off the fire.

4. While the *kababs* are cooking, cut the onion in rings. You can ask an adult to help you with this. If you are allowed to do it yourself, first peel the onion. Set it on the counter top with the broad side down, hold steady with your left hand and slice into as thin rings as possible.
   Put the rings in the small bowl and pour over just enough vinegar to cover them. Cover and keep aside. These onions are really delicious if you can leave them like this, soaking in the vinegar for at least 4-5 hours. They turn a light pink. If you don't have the time or better said, are too hungry to wait, use them as they are.

5. Slice the rolls lengthwise. Butter them. Into each, put one *kabab* and some onion rings. Hold down with a toothpick.

BURGER BONANZA

Were some of you upset that you couldn't try out the last recipe because you're vegetarian? Well, in that case, cheer up. Here's something specially for you—choose which kind of burger you feel like having and have a feast. By the way, if you're offering to make some for friends or family remember to take the order stylishly. Ask which burger they'll have—a *Tikki* Burger? a Tomato and Cheese Burger? a Mint-Potato Burger?
Go on, have fun.

You Will Need For EACH Tikki Burger

1 burger bun
1 *Tikki* (see recipe in the section on Snacks)
butter
tomato sauce

onion rings, if you like (see how to make them in the last recipe)
a tooth-pick

You Will Also Need

a knife, a chopping board, a small bowl if you're making the onion rings

To Make It

1. Slice the bun. Butter it on both sides and then pour some tomato sauce on each half and spread it neatly to the edges.
2. Onto one half, put a *tikki*. I'm sure you would

157

have made them well and asked an adult to help you fry them. By the way, whenever you do make *tikkis*, why not make a few extra and enjoy these burgers the next day.

3. Top each *tikki* with a few slices of onion, if you're using them.
4. Top with the other half of the bun. Hold it down with a tooth-pick.
5. Sink your teeth into it!

TIKKI BURGER WITH CHEESE

Before you close your *tikki* burger (the one we just made), slip in a slice of cheese or instead of the butter, use cheese spread.

SWEET SOUR *TIKKI* BURGER

Spread Tamrind chutney (see recipe for *Alu Papri Chaat*) onto the butter and then top with the *tikki*. In this case, don't use the tomato sauce.

TOMATO CHEESE BURGER

Instead of the *tikki*, fill your bun with a slice of tomato, a slice of cheese and if you like capsicum, a slice of capsicum. Also, if you like mustard, it does go very well with this burger. Spread a little onto the bun halves before you fill them.

SAUCY NOODLES

Do you like these tomatoey-cheesy Noodles? You do?
So do I. Should we make some today?

You Will Need For TWO People

100 grams noodles	3 tablespoons tomato sauce
3 cups water	a dash of chilli sauce, if you
3 tomatoes	want to make them spicy
2 cloves garlic	$1/2$–1 teaspoon salt
2 tablespoons oil	1 cup water
1 green chilli, if you like,	some cheese (not essential)

You Will Also Need

a medium sized pan with a lid, a blender, a knife, a
spoon to stir, a grater, if you're using cheese, a large
strainer, oven gloves, a *karhai*.

To Make It

1. First, let's boil the noodles. Put the water in
   the pan and the pan on the fire. Cover it and
   let the water start boiling.
2. Drop in the noodles along with a few drops of
   oil. Cover and keep the heat on high till the
   water starts boiling again which will happen
   in a few seconds. Turn the heat down to
   medium and cook for about 6 minutes.
3. Wear your oven gloves. Take the pan off the fire.
   and holding the strainer over the sink, pour
   the noodles into it so the water can drain away.

It's hot and steamy when you do this so ask for help. Hold the strainer under cold water for a minute.

4. While the noodles are cooking, you can wash the tomatoes and chop them into 4 pieces each. Put them into the blender and whizz for a minute till they're a smooth paste. You can also peel the garlic. If you find it hard to do, drop it into water for a little while and then try again—the skins should slip off easily. Now, if you're good with a knife, chop them into little pieces. If you're not, just crush it by banging with a rolling pin. Chop the green chilli if you're using it.

5. Now let's make the sauce. Put the oil in the *karhai* on a medium flame. Let it heat up for a few minutes.

6. Drop in the garlic. Stir and after a few seconds, add the tomato paste, the sauces and salt. You can also drop in the green chilli. Stir for a minute, then add the 1 cup of water and cover the *karhai*. Let it cook on a slow fire for 10 minutes.

7. Carefully, wearing the oven gloves again, lift up the cover and pour in the boiled noodles. Stir them around, cover the pan and let them cook in the sauce for another 4-5 minutes or till the sauce is as thick as you want it. Of course, you can wait that long!

8. If you're eating immediately, serve yourself and grate some cheese over the noodles. If you're going to eat much later, pour the noodles into an oven-proof dish. Grate some cheese over the top. When you're ready to eat, heat the dish in an oven pre-heated to 180°c for about 15 minutes.

BAKED STRIPES

You will love this—stripes of all the things you enjoy. Just look at the recipe—there are noodles in it and baked beans and some cheese and of course, you can change the stripes as you like. Sounds exciting? It is.

You Will Need For SIX People

150 grams noodles
$^1/_2$–1 teaspoon salt
1 large tin baked beans
200 grams cottage cheese
(*paneer*)

2 capsicums,
2 cubes cheese

You Will Also Need

a largeish pan to boil the noodles, a plate, an oven-proof dish, a tin-opener, a grater, a knife, a chopping board, oven gloves, a timer

To Make It

1. Boil the noodles. You can look back to the recipe for Saucy Noodles to see how it's done. Sprinkle over the salt and mix it in.
2. Open the tin of baked beans.
3. Grate the cottage cheese into a plate. Use the grater to do it.
4. Chop the capsicums or slice them into rings. Use the chopping board and knife to do it.

161

5. Now you're ready to make the stripes. Drop a teaspoon of oil into the oven-proof dish and rub all over the bottom with your finger. Now put in half the noodles, then a stripe of half the beans, the half the capsicum, then half the grated *paneer*, then grate some of the cubed cheese over. Make the same stripes again, starting with the noodles and finishing up all the ingredients.

6. To bake the dish, set the oven on to pre-heat to 180°c. Wearing your oven gloves, put the dish in. Set the timer for 35 minutes. When you peek in when the timer rings, the dish should be bubbly hot and the cheese on top a golden brown. Serve immediately.

Note: If there is left-over cooked mince (*keema*) in the fridge, add a stripe of it too.

CHICKEN IN TOMATO SAUCE

Doesn't this just sound like a mouth-watering recipe? It is—a grilled chicken coated with tomato sauce that you will enjoy cooking and gobbling up. Try it on your family or friends—I bet it will make you even more popular than you already are!

You Will Need For 8 Single Piece Servings

1 chicken, cut into 8 pieces
$^1/_2$ cup tomato sauce, either plain or flavoured with garlic or chilli
juice of $^1/_2$ lemon
some pepper

$^1/_2$ teaspoon sugar
3 tablespoons oil
$^3/_4$ teaspoon salt

You Will Also Need

a fork, a plate, a small bowl, a pastry brush or large-sized paint-brush, a spoon, an oven-proof dish with a lid or some foil, oven gloves, a timer.

To Make It

1. Wash the chicken well. Ask an adult for help if you need. Throw away the bits that are not needed. Again you may need to ask for help. Put the washed pieces in a plate.
2. Now poke each piece of chicken all over with the fork.
3. In the bowl, mix together the sauce, lemon

163

juice, sugar, oil, salt and pepper. As for the pepper, add just as much as you like—$^{1}/_{2}$ teaspoon or more. This is your 'paint'.

4. Use the pastry brush or your paint-brush (it should be new or very, very clean) to paint thickly all over each piece of chicken. As you finish, lay each piece in the oven-proof dish. If there is any sauce left over, pour it over the pieces. If you have time, let the pieces sit in the sauce for a few hours.

5. When you are ready to cook, set the oven on to preheat to 180°c. Put the lid (or foil) over the dish. Wear your oven gloves. Put the dish into the oven. Set the timer for 45 minutes. Check on the chicken by again wearing your gloves and poking at the chicken with a fork. If it is not done. keep it in the oven for another 10 minutes. Serve immediately, and why not make a nice salad to go with it?

Note: By the way, this chicken is not a dry one. It has a thin sauce in the dish when it finishes cooking. If, however, you want to make it grilled, you can do that too. It is delicious. All you do is for the last ten minutes of cooking time, remove the lid(or foil) and let some of the liquid dry up. The chicken will get a nice crunchy outer.

Along with the salad, how about asking an adult in your family to fry you some chips to go with your chicken? Doesn't it sound like a dream meal?

CHIPSY CHICKEN

Weren't we just talking about chicken and chips and licking our lips? Well, here's another amazing recipe. All your favourite things again!

You Will Need For 8 Single Piece Servings

1 chicken, cut into
eight pieces
$^1/_2$ cup butter
pepper

salt
1 large packet of your
favourite chips

You Will Also Need

a fork, 2 plates, a small pan with a handle, a pastry brush or large, clean paint-brush, a rolling pin, an oven-proof dish, oven gloves, a timer.

To Make It

1. Set the oven on to preheat to 180°c.
2. Wash the chicken pieces well. Ask an adult for help if you need. Throw away the bits that are not needed. Ask for help again. Lay the washed pieces on the plate.
3. Poke each piece all over with a fork.
4. Set the butter in the handled pan on the fire for a few minutes till it melts.
5. Snip open the chip packet and keeping the chips in the packet itself, beat lightly with the rolling pin to break into crumbs. You can crush

them with your hand if you prefer. Lay the crumbs on the second plate.

6. With the pastry brush or fork, paint all the pieces of chicken with the melted butter. Sprinkle a little pepper and salt over each.

7. As you finish painting each piece, drop it into the plate with the chip-crumbs. Press down lightly so that the crumbs stick to the chicken. Crumb both sides of the chicken and keep laying the pieces in the oven-proof dish. Try not to let them touch each other.

8. When the oven is heated up, wearing your oven gloves, put the dish into the oven. Set the timer to 45 minutes. Check on the chicken when the timer rings. You may need an adult to help you decide whether it's done or needs 10 minutes more.

9. Serve immediately. If you have any chip-crumbs left over, sprinkle them over just before serving.

Note: For an interesting change, you can grate some cheese over the chicken in the last ten minutes of cooking time. Of course, you will be very careful when you are handling the hot dish, taking it out of the oven and then putting it back.

SIMPLE SPICY CHICKEN

Here's another easy chicken you can offer to make—
and your mother might ask you for the recipe later!

You Will Need For 8 Single Piece Servings

1 medium sized chicken,
cut into 8 pieces
4 tablespoons slightly sour
curds
juice of 1 small lemon
5 cloves garlic

1 small piece ginger, about
$1^1/_2$" in length
red chilli powder, if you like
1 teaspoon coriander
powder (dhaniya)
$1-1^1/_2$ teaspoons salt
4 tablespoons oil

You Will Also Need

a bowl, a chopping board, a karhai with a lid, a fork,
a blender or mixi

To Make It

1. Wash the chicken well and throw away any bits
   you don't need. Ask an adult for help to do this.
2. Peel and wash the garlic and ginger. To make
   it easier to peel the garlic, you can leave it in a
   small bowl of water for 15 minutes and you
   will find the skins skip off easily. For the ginger,
   first peel it using a vegetable peeler then wash
   it and cut it into slices or bits before putting it
   into the blender. Grind it to a paste with the
   garlic in the blender or mixi.

167

3. Mix together in the bowl the curds, lime-juice, garlic, ginger, chilli powder, coriander powder and salt.

4. On the chopping board, prick each piece of chicken all over with the fork. Into each, rub some of the curds mixture you have made in the bowl. When all the pieces are done, drop them into the same bowl and leave it aside for at least an hour and for 3-4 hours if you have time. If it is summer, keep it in the fridge.

5. When you're ready to cook, put the *karhai* onto the fire over a medium flame. Pour in the oil and after a few minutes, the chicken with all its juices. Cover the pan and cook on a slow fire for at least half an hour. If you peep into the pan after about ten minutes, you will see lots of liquid in the pan. After another ten minutes, it will start to dry up. If the chicken starts sticking to the bottom of the pan at this stage, you will have to keep stirring it around. In another ten minutes, the chicken should be tender, the juices will be gone and the chicken should get lightly fried in the oil remaining in the pan. Remember those onion rings we made for our Seekh Kabab Surprises? Serve the chicken with the same ones sprinkled over.

PEA PULLAO

If you're deciding to make this, I must say you're well on the way to becoming a dedicated cook! Now you can go on and follow almost any recipe and continue adding to your collection. Of course, this *pullao* is best made when the peas are fresh but you can also make it with frozen ones.

You Will Need For FOUR People

1^1/$_2$ cups good quality rice	3 onions
4 tablespoons oil	1^1/$_2$ cups shelled peas
1 teaspoon cumin (*zeera*)	1 teaspoon salt

You Will Also Need

a large, flat, heavy-bottomed pan with a tight-fitting lid, a griddle (*tava*), a chopping board, a knife, a stirring spoon, a plastic bowl, a large plate to pick the rice, oven gloves

To Make It

1. Pick the rice—that means remove from it any little bits of rubbish. Ask an adult to show you how to do it. Now wash the rice well in many changes of water. This is how you do it. Pour the rice into a plastic bowl. Pour water over, rub the rice with your hand, pour the water out and repeat till the water looks clear (it well look whitish when you start). Pour 3

169

cups clean, boiled water over the rice. Leave it to soak for at least half an hour.

2. While the rice is soaking, go on with the other preparations. First let's get over the more difficult task of slicing the onions. Peel them. Drop them into water, then slice thinly. Reading through the first few pages should help you.

3. To cook, put the large pan on the fire. Pour in the oil. Heat for 5 minutes.

4. Drop in the cumin. Let it fry for a few seconds. It will turn a shade darker.

5. Drop in the onions. Stir them around on a medium flame till they brown—a nice golden brown.

6. Add the peas and salt. Stir and fry for another few minutes.

7. Add the rice along with the water in which it has been soaking.

8. Cover the pan, raise the heat to high and let the liquids come to a boil. They might come rushing out of the pan—just take the lid off and they will go back down again. Be careful when you do this—the pan is hot. Use your oven gloves.
Let the liquids boil down to the level of the rice, then cover the pan tightly, put the *tava* underneath it and keep on a slow fire for 20 minutes. Set the timer on to remind you.

9. When you peep in, (use your gloves again and be careful! there's hot steam coming out of the pan) you will see little holes over the top of the rice. That means it is cooked fully. You can test a grain by taking one out with a spoon and crushing it between your fingers.

10. Serve your pullao immediately, making sure to mix the rice and peas well.

11. A *raita* served with the pullao makes a complete meal.

Note: This, by the way, is the simplest pullao. You can vary it by adding whole spices—cinnamon (*dalchini*), cloves (*laung*), black pepper and cardamom (*elaichi*) along with the cumin (*zeera*). Also, if you like, you can add ground ginger and garlic (1 teaspoon of each should be enough) along with the onions. For a total change, instead of peas, use other vegetables—potatoes, cauliflower, carrots.

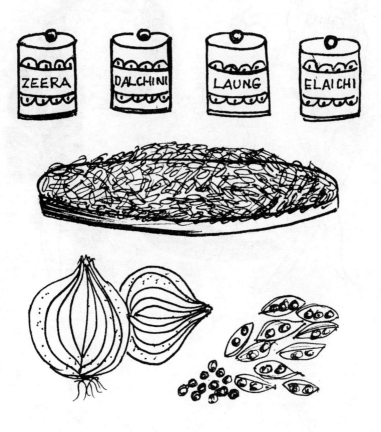

SALADS AND RAITAS

H ere are all those little extras that will go to make your meal complete—*raitas* and salads. As I mentioned in the last chapter, you can team them with *pullaos* and burgers and chicken or you know, you can have a salad just by itself, specially in the hot summer months when your appetite is not at its hungriest. That goes for *raitas* too. In fact, there are days when you feel like having nothing more than a big bowlful of well-chilled *raita*. If it's one with potatoes in it, for example, it can be quite filling too. So, try out all these things. Even if you're not making a whole meal, perhaps you could contribute just one of these dishes to the lunch or dinner table. Why not?

ALU RAITA
(Curds with Potatoes)

Do you like *Alu Raita*? I can have bowlfuls of it, nice and cold and filling. You can make it for your family too.

You Will Need For FOUR People

3 medium potatoes
$2^1/_2$ cups curds
$^1/_2$ teaspoon salt
$^3/_4$-1 teaspoon cumin (*zeera*) powder

$^1/_2$-1 teaspoon sugar
a green chilli or red chilli powder, if you like

You Will Also Need

a bowl to beat the curds, an egg-beater, a pressure cooker to boil the potatoes, a chopping board and knife if you're using the green chilli.

To Make It

1. Wash and scrub the potatoes nicely. Boil them. (You can see how to do this if you look at the recipe for *Channa Chaat*). When they are done, take them out of the cooker and keep them aside to cool completely.
2. When you are ready to make the *raita*, put the curds into the bowl and lightly beat it up with the egg-beater till it is smooth. Add to it the salt, *zeera*, sugar and chilli powder. If you're

175

using the green chilli, of course, you have to chop it up into little bits—I'm sure you know how to do that by now. Mix well. With a clean spoon, taste a little bit—add more sugar, salt or *zeera* if it's needed.

3. Peel the potatoes and cube them into small bits. Of course, you know how to do that too. Haven't you made *Alu Chaat* dozens of times by now? As you keep cutting them, drop them into the curds. Mix up well and put into the fridge to chill.

Note: If there is any left-over mint chutney in the fridge, stir in a few teaspoons into the curds. *Mmmm...* it's delicious. If there's no ground chutney, but mint is in season, chop or tear it into little bits and mix that into the curds instead.

GAJAR KA RAITA
(Curds with Carrots)

Another fantastic combination—and it's orange in colour this time. I think you'll enjoy it, specially when the carrots are fresh and juicy.

You Will Need For FOUR People

1 large carrot or two smaller ones
$1/2$ teaspoon cumin (*zeera*) powder
$2^1/_2$ cups curds
a green chilli, finely
$1/2$ teaspoon salt
chopped, if you like

You Will Also Need

a vegetable peeler, a grater, a plate, a bowl to beat the curds, an egg-beater, a knife and chopping board if you're using the green chilli

To Make It

1. Wash the carrot well. With the potato peeler, peel it lightly. Wash it again.
2. Now you can grate the carrot. This you're getting really good at, aren't you? Use the grater to do it and let it fall into the plate. About a cupful will be enough.
3. Put the curds into the bowl in which you're planning to beat it. Beat it smooth with the egg-beater, adding the salt, *zeera* and chilli as you go along. Taste a little with a clean spoon and see if you need to add more of anything.

4. Put in the grated carrot. Mix. it well with the curds and put it into the fridge to chill well before you sample it.

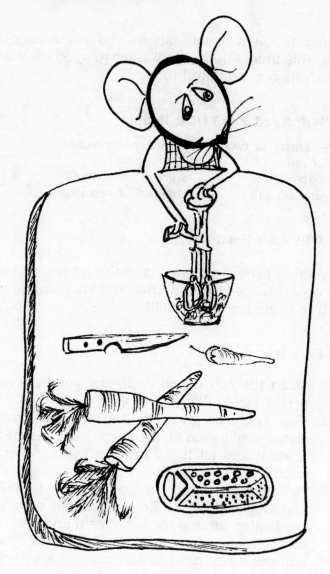

KHEERE KA RAITA

(Curds with Cucumber)

Is this pale green *raita*, nicely chilled, just what you fed like helping yourself to on a hot summer's day? It's good for you too, have some more!

You Will Need for FOUR People

1 small cucumber
2 $^1/_2$ cups curds
$^1/_2$ teaspoon salt
$^1/_2$ - $^3/_4$ teaspoon sugar

a little black pepper
a green chilli or red chilli powder (if you like)

You Will Also Need

a vegetable peeler, a grater, a knife, a plate, a bowl to beat the curds, an egg-beater, a knife and chopping board to chop the chilli. if you're using if

To Make It

1. First, we've got to prepare the cucumber. You know how bitter it can be. So, to cure it off that, cut off a little cap from the stem side. With the knife, make a cross on the cut bit of the cucumber. Rub with the cap—a white froth will come out. When it stops, you can stop too. Cut off a thin slice of cucumber where you 'treated' it. Peel the skin off, with the vegetable peeler. Now grate the cucumber, using the

179

vegetable grater. If you've forgotten how to make the best use of these gadgets, the first few pages of the book will help you remember. Grate the cucumber into the plate. Sprinkle a little salt over it and leave it aside for about ten minutes.

2. Meanwhile, you can get the curds ready. Put it into the bowl in which you will beat it. Add the salt, sugar, pepper and chilli, if you're using it. Beat with the egg-beater till it's smooth.

3. Now look back at the cucumber. You might see it sitting in a little pool of water. Drain it away by tilting the plate. Hold the cucumber back to stop it slipping away too. Add it to the beaten curds and mix it in well. Put it in the fridge to chill well before helping yourself to a cool bowlful.

Note: To this recipe too, as to the last one. you can add some finely chopped or torn up mint, when it's in season.

TRI-COLOURED RAITA

Yes, its orange, green and white, this tricoloured—hey, its not the national flag I'm talking about, its a new kind of *raita* in just those three colours. Be sure to make it on Independence Day!

You Will Need For FOUR People

1 small cucumber
1 small carrot
2$^1/_2$ cups curds
$^1/_2$ teaspoon salt
$^1/_2$–1 teaspoon sugar

$^3/_4$ teaspoon cumin (*zeera*) powder
a green chilli. finely chopped (if you like)

You Will Also Need

a vegetable peeler, a grater, two plates, a bowl to beat the curds, an egg-beater, a knife and chopping board to chop up the chilli, if you're using it.

To Make It

1. Wash the carrot well. With the vegetable peeler, peel it lightly. Wash it again. Using the grater, grate it into one of the plates.
2. Prepare the cucumber as we did for the cucumber *raita*. That means you have to cut a cap off, rub it well, peel it and then grate it into the second plate, Sprinkle a little salt over it and keep it aside.
3. Put the curds into the bowl in which you're

181

going to beat it. Add the salt, sugar, cumin, the chilli, if you're using it and beat it smooth.

4. Drop in the carrot and the cucumber. In the case of the cucumber, drain away any water it might be sitting in before you add it.

5. Mix your special tricoloured *raita* well before you put it into the fridge to chill thoroughly.

MOOLI RAITA

(Curds With Radish)

Don't tell me you won't try this recipe because you don't like radish? It's not my favourite too but it is just so delicious combined with curds. You will enjoy it teamed it with *parathas*, or a *pullao*.

You Will Need For FOUR People

1 medium sized white radish
$2^1/_2$ cups curds
$^1/_2$ teaspoon salt
$^1/_2 - ^3/_4$ teaspoon sugar

$^3/_4$ teaspoon cumin (*zeera*) powder
a green chilli, finely chopped if you like

You Will Also Need

a vegetable peeler, a grater, a plate, a bowl to beat the curds, an egg-beater, a knife and chopping board to chop the chilli, if you're using it.

To Make It

1. Wash the radish well. With the vegetable peeler, peel it lightly. Wash it again.
2. Grate the radish using the grater. ($^3/_4$ cup should be enough). Let it drop onto the plate kept below. Sprinkle it with a little salt and keep it aside.
3. Put the curds into the bowl in which you are planning to beat it. Beat it smooth with the

183

egg-beater, adding the salt, sugar, cumin and chilli, if you're using it. Taste a little with a clean spoon and see if you need to add anything more.

4. Put in the radish. Take as much as you can hold in your hand. Squeeze it gently and drop it into the curds. Do it to all the radish.

5. Mix the curds well and keep it in the fridge to chill well before eating.

CURDS WITH SPROUTS

This must certainly be my favourite *raita*. It's full of protein and energy too. I'm sorry if I sound like an advertisement for some health-food but that's exactly what this is!

You Will Need For FOUR People

$^3/_4$ cup sprouts*
$2^1/_2$ cups curds
$^1/_2$ teaspoon salt

$^3/_4$–1 teaspoon sugar
$^1/_2$ teaspoon *Chaat Masala*
a green chilli, finely chopped, if you like

You Will Also Need

a bowl to beat the curds, an egg-beater, a knife and chopping board to chop the chilli if you're using it, a bowl and napkin to make the sprouts

To Make It

1. Put the curds into the bowl in which you're planning to beat it. Add the salt, sugar, *Chaat Masala* and chilli, if you're using it.
2. Add the sprouts and mix together well with the curds.
3. Taste a little bit with a clean spoon and see if you need to add anything more. Perfect it and put it into the fridge to chill well. Isn't the crunch of the sprouts and the coolness of the curds a delicious combination?

---

*You can see how to make them in the recipe for Full-of-Energy Sprouts.

185

MACARONI SALAD

Do you like macaroni? How about trying out this easy salad? You will need an adult to help you make the mayonnnaise or you could buy some from the market and you're all set to go.

You Will Need For FOUR People

1 cup macaroni	$^1/_2$–$^3/4$ cup mayonnaise
3 cups water	2 tablespoons tomato sauce
1 cube cheese*	$^1/_2$ teaspoon salt
1 big capsicum	$^1/_2$ teaspoon pepper

You Will Also Need

a large pan to boil the macaroni, a grater, a knife and chopping board, a serving bowl, a large spoon, a strainer, oven-gloves.

To Make It

1. First, let's boil the macaroni. Put the water into the large pan. Set it on the fire. As soon as it comes to a boil, drop the macaroni in. Be careful as you do it. Let the gas remain on high till the water comes to a boil again. This will happen in a few seconds. Reduce the heat and keep it on the fire for 6 minutes.

---

*Don't worry if you don't have a cube. Grate about 4 tablespoons of any cheese.

2. Wear your oven gloves. Put the fire off and take the pan to the sink. Hold the strainer in your gloved hand and pour the macaroni into it. You might need some help. As soon as the water has run through, hold the strainer under the cold water tap for a few seconds. Leave it over any pan to drain, for a few minutes.

3. While the macaroni is still hot, pour it into the serving dish. Grate the cheese over and stir in.

4. Wash the capsicum and chop it up. Cut it lengthwise into half, then into strips. Remove all the white seeds and chop the strips into little bits.

5. Drop in the chopped capsicum and also the mayonnaise, sauce, salt and pepper. Mix everything together well and chill before serving.

---

*Don't worry if you don't have a cube. Crate about 4 tablespoons of any cheese

POTATO-PINEAPPLE SALAD

Another irresistible combination. Potatoes and pineapple. Again, you need an adult's help to make the mayonnaise unless you decide to buy some from the market and go ahead on your own.

You Will Need For FOUR People

3 big potatoes   1 small tin pineapple slices*
about 1/2 cup mayonnaise

You Will Also Need

a pressure cooker to boil the potatoes, a knife, a chopping board, a tin-opener, a serving dish, a tablespoon

To Make It

1. As we did for the *Channa Chaat*, first we have to boil the potatoes. Once they are done, keep them away and let them cool completely. Peel them and cut them into pieces. Use the chopping board and knife to do it. Put the chopped potatoes into the serving dish.
2. Pour the mayonnaise over the potatoes and mix it up well. Just put in as much as coats the potatoes nicely.

---

*You can eat the left-over ones, of course or use them in the Sprouts Salad at the end of the section.

3. Open the pineapple tin. Take out 3 of the slices. Chop them also into small pieces with the knife. Drop them into the bowl with the potatoes and mix in well. Also add a tablespoon of the pineapple syrup. Taste a little spoonful and see if anything is needed—you might need a little salt. If it's just fine, put it into the fridge, covered with a plate. Let it sit there till you're ready to eat.

4. Just before serving, mix well.

    This salad goes well with some of the chicken meals mentioned in the last chapter as well as with the Saucy Noodles. You can also use it to fill a burger.

COLD POTATO SALAD

This salad is very versatile—that means you can use it in many ways. You can eat a bowlful of it by itself when you're feeling hungry, you can serve it with a pizza or one of those chicken dishes or you can just make a meal of it served with a soup and a hot toast. Of course, if you decide to do that, remember to boil at least 6 potatoes instead of 4.

You Will Need For FOUR People

4 big potatoes
For The Dressing*

$^1/_2$ cup cooking oil
2 tablespoons white vinegar
1 teaspoon sugar
$^1/_2$ teaspoon salt
$^1/_2$–1 teaspoon black pepper

$^1/_2$ teaspoon dry mustard powder or $^3/_4$ teaspoon made mustard
1 tablespoon tomato sauce
2 cloves garlic, if you like
$^1/_2$ teaspoon red chilli powder, if you like

You Will Also Need

a pressure cooker to boil the potatoes, a clean glass jar with a well-fitting lid, a big spoon, a measuring cup, a knife and chopping board, a serving bowl.

To Make It

1. Boil the potatoes. You know how to do it by

*Of course, you will not need all this quantity for 1 recipe but it is useful to make and keep away.

now, I'm sure. If you don't, look in the recipe for *Channa Chaat*. As for the *chaat*, it is best to boil the potatoes much earlier and leave them to cool before you peel them and cube them into pieces. Use the knife and chopping board to do it.

2. To make the dressing, put all the things required for it into the glass jar and shake it up well. You will need to peel and chop the garlic. Put it into the fridge till you need to use it. It is best to make it in advance too so that the flavour of the mustard comes through.

3. After you cube the potatoes, pour some of the dressing over them. Mix well—the potatoes should look neither too dry nor should they be floating in the dressing. So use just as much as you need and keep the rest away to use another time. Just before serving, add an extra tablespoonfull and mix well. Put into a pretty serving bowl before you put it on the table.

CUCUMBER SALAD WITH PEANUTS

Here's another of my favourite recipes—chilled cucumber with crunchy peanuts, dressed with lemon and a sprinkling of roasted sesame. Its a really super combination.

You Will Need For FOUR People

2 big cucumbers or 3 small ones $^1/_4$ teaspoon salt
$1^1/_2$ teaspoons sesame (*til*) $^1/_4$ teaspoon pepper
$^1/_2$ lemon
2 tablespoons peanuts

You Will Also Need

a griddle (*tava*), a knife, a chopping board, a potato peeler, a lemon squeezer, a serving bowl

To Make It

1. First, lets treat the cucumbers, as we did for the cucumber *raita*. When you have them peeled and washed, cube them. To cube them, cut the cucumber into half, lengthwise. Now cut the halves again lengthwise and then cut the strips you have into bits. Put into a bowl and leave in the fridge.

2. To prepare for your salad treat, you have to do one more thing now. Put the *tava* onto the fire, let it heat up for a few minutes then drop the

192

til onto it. Take a spoon and shake it around gently. Soon it will get light brown. Take the *tava* off the fire and put the *til* into a bowl. If you feel like it, you can ask an adult for help to do this step of the recipe.

3. When you're ready to serve the salad, run into the kitchen, put the chilled cucumber into the serving bowl, add the juice from the lemon, the salt, pepper, peanuts and finally, the *til.* Quickly, mix at all up and serve immediately.

Don't you love the crunch and flavour? I do too.

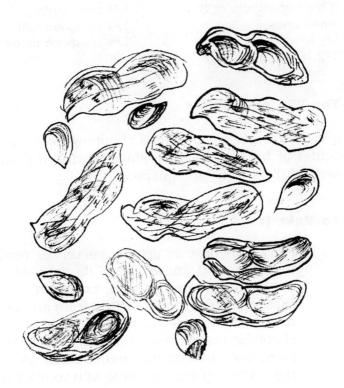

SPECIAL CUCUMBER SALAD

This is just such an easy to make yet special salad. It has a secret dressing—honey and lemon mixed together. You will enjoy making and serving it again and again.

You Will Need For FOUR People

2 big cucumbers or 3 small ones
$1/2$ lemon
1–2 teaspoons honey

1/4 cup curds
1/4 teaspoon salt
1/4 teaspoon pepper

You Will Also Need

a vegetable peeler, a knife, a chopping board, an egg beater or big metal spoon, small bowl to dressing, a serving dish, a lemon squeezer

To Make It

1. First, you have to get the cucumber ready to be eaten. You know how to do that—like you did for the cucumber *raita*, except that in this case, after removing the bitter froth and peeling the cucumber, don't grate it. Place it on the chopping board, hold it steady with your left hand and cut into thin round slices with your right. Those of you who write with your left hand, can reverse hands. Put the sliced cucumber into the serving bowl and into the fridge.

194

2. Make the dressing. Using the lemon squeezer, squeeze the lemon into the bowl. Be careful to remove any seeds that may drop in. Add to it the honey, curds, salt and pepper. With the egg beater, or spoon, beat the curds smooth. Taste a little spoonful and add more salt or honey if it's needed. It should taste nicely sweet and sour. Put this too into the fridge.
3. Just before serving, pour the dressing over the cucumber and mix it in well. Now take a test-bite!

FULL-OF-ENERGY SPROUTS

This is really a fantastic salad to make. Sprouts need no cooking to sprout and once they're done, you can dress them simply with lemon and salt and you're ready to eat a plateful of energy.

You Will Need For FOUR People

1³/₄ cups Green gram
(*Sabut Moong Dal*)*
1–2 green chillies, if you like

2 lemons
¹/₂–³/₄ teaspoon salt
Chaat Masala, if you like

You Will Also Need

a bowl to soak the gram, a plate, a clean napkin, a lemon squeezer, a chopping board and knife if you're using the chillies

To Make It

1. Lets have some fun to start with. Let's sprout the Gram. Put it into the bowl, and wash it well. Change the water a number of times then pour in enough water to cover the Gram and leave it in a warm place. Cover it with a plate. After 6–8 hours, drain away the water, wet the napkin and put it over the Gram. Leave it for at least another 10 hours. By this time, when you look at your Gram, it should have sprouted.

---

*This is the *dal* that looks like small, green, circular stones.

That means it will have little white roots coming out of it. Taste one—it will taste crunchy. Of course, you can eat them now but if you want longer roots, leave them for another day.

2. Wash and chop the green chillies finely if you're using them. Add them to the sprouts.
3. To dress the sprouts, squeeze the lemon juice over, using the squeezer. Add the juice of 1 lemon first, mix it in well, taste it and decide if you need more and how much. Also add the salt and pepper and *Chaat Masala*. With the masala too, add a teaspoon, mix it then taste to see if you need more.
4. Keep the salad in the fridge till you're ready to eat it.

Apart from eating sprouts as a salad, you can try eating them on toast too. You can also try adding little pineapple or fresh apple bits to the salad. Boiled potatoes too are a good idea. Left-over sprouts in fact can be added to any salad—cucumber, tomato, cabbage or a mixture of them all.

GOODBYE AND HELLO

Well, that brings us to the end of the book. I hope you've enjoyed cooking through it and by now, have some of the reicpes marked out as your favourites. As I prepare to say Goodbye to you, I do hope this book will be your 'Hello' to the exciting hobby of cooking. I hope that by now you have started enjoying being in the kitchen and feel inspired enough to collect more recipes of your own. You can get them from friends who have cooked something that you have enjoyed eating or from other books and magazines. Make a notebook for yourself. You can start rightaway, of course, in these pages that have been left for you.

Another tip I'd like to share with you: When you try a recipe, write a little note to yourself below it, saying how you liked it, or whether you might change it in some way to make it even better the next time round. Perhaps there was some detail in it that the.author hadn't mentioned which you feel you want to remember—write that down too. Then you will gradually build up a collection of really useful and fool-proof recipes.

Good Luck. As I said at the beginning, Congratulations! You've got yourself a ticket to fun. Make the most of it.

MY OWN RECIPES

_____

_____

_____

_____

_____

_____

_____

_____

_____

_____

_____

_____

_____

_____

_____